W9-ABC-797

Mastering CDA Competencies

Using
Working with Young Children

by
Dr. Judy Herr
Professor, Early Childhood Education
College of Human Development
University of Wisconsin–Stout
Menomonie, Wisconsin

Publisher
The Goodheart-Willcox Company, Inc.
Tinley Park, Illinois

Copyright © 2004

by

THE GOODHEART-WILLCOX COMPANY, INC.

Previous Editions Copyright 2002, 1998, 1994, 1990

All rights reserved. No part of this book may be reproduced, stored in a retrieval system, or transmitted in any form or by any means, electronic, mechanical, photocopying, recording, or otherwise, without the prior written permission of The Goodheart-Willcox Company, Inc. Manufactured in the United States of America.

International Standard Book Number 1-59070-155-0

2 3 4 5 6 7 8 9 0   04   09 08 07 06 05

Acknowledgments

The following professionals reviewed the text and provided valuable input:

Barbara Diaz-Caneja
Child Development Specialist
U.S. Air Force Child Development Program
San Antonio, Texas

Mary Doidge
Chair
Child Development Department
Des Moines Area Community College
Ankeny, Iowa

Wendy Nielsen
Director of Professional Services
Resources for Child Caring
St. Paul, Minnesota

Vera F. Spraggins
Associate Professor
Early Childhood Education and Development
St. Petersburg Junior College
St. Petersburg, Florida

Neysa Stevenson-Laux
Child Care Apprenticeship Coordinator
Pinellas Technical Education Center
Clearwater, Florida

Jessie M. Zola
Instructor
University of Wisconsin-Milwaukee
Milwaukee, Wisconsin

Contents

Part 4
Learning Experiences for Children

Part 5
Other People You Will Meet

Appendix

Introduction

Promoting children's growth in a child care setting is an exciting career opportunity. Congratulations! Earning your Child Development Associate Credential will enable you to meet children's needs; nurture their physical, social, emotional, and cognitive development; and work cooperatively with parents and other adults to ensure excellent early childhood education.

The CDA program represents a national effort to credential qualified caregivers who work with children age zero to five years. After successfully completing this program, you will join other professionals who have received their CDA Credential by mastering the CDA Competency Goals and Functional Areas.

The CDA program uses six statements of skill called Competency Goals to establish the framework for caregiver behavior. These goals are divided into 13 Functional Areas, which describe major tasks caregivers must accomplish to satisfy the Competency Goals. Study the chart in this Introduction. It outlines the Competency Goals, Functional Areas, and chapters to which they correspond in this book and in *Working with Young Children*. Then it's up to you to master them, using this book to complete your fieldwork, course work, or assessment successfully.

Students may earn the CDA Credential in one of two ways: by the Professional Preparation Program or by Direct Assessment. Read on for a brief description of both. However, for detailed information, contact the Council for Professional Recognition, which manages the CDA program. Staff can answer your questions or forward program literature. Contact them at the following location:

Council for Professional Recognition
2460 16th Street, NW
Washington, DC 20009
(800) 424-4310
(202) 265-9090
FAX (202) 265-9161
cdacouncil.org

Mastering CDA Competencies Through the Professional Preparation Program

Mastering CDA Competencies can help you earn your CDA through the Professional Preparation Program. It successfully prepares you for the three phases you must complete to receive your credential.

Fieldwork

To complete the CDA fieldwork requirement, you'll work or volunteer in a child care setting. You will complement this experience by reading the text *Working with Young Children* and completing coordinating chapters in *Mastering CDA Competencies*. A field advisor will guide you through your classroom experiences; tie them to textbook lessons that focus on early childhood education; and use *Mastering CDA Competencies* to turn lessons into practical learning experiences.

Course Work

To fulfill your course work requirement, you will attend 120 hours of group seminars with other candidates. A seminar instructor will discuss the eight formal education areas, then administer a written examination to evaluate your knowledge at the end of the course work.

Final Evaluation

The final evaluation completes your training. *Mastering CDA Competencies* can help you prepare a Professional Resource File and Parent Opinion Questionnaires. When you have completed the assignments in this book, you may include some of them as part of your Professional Resource File. *Mastering CDA Competencies* also includes a copy of the parent questionnaire in the Appendix. You can photocopy and distribute this questionnaire to the parents of children in your care. After compiling these items, you will complete a series of exercises to demonstrate your early childhood skills. A CDA representative will interview and evaluate your competence, then submit results to the Council for Early Childhood Professional Recognition. Successful candidates will receive the CDA Credential.

Together, *Mastering CDA Competencies* and *Working with Young Children* will help you obtain the CDA Credential. This comprehensive text addresses child development, proceeds to developmentally appropriate and effective curricula, and concludes with professional concerns, such as working with parents and finding employment. Early childhood principles and CDA Competency Goals are covered in a logical order. *Mastering CDA Competencies* translates textbook information into practical observations and exercises. The combination of comprehensive reading and practical application will enable you to master early childhood principles, earn your CDA Credential, and become a competent caregiver.

Mastering CDA Competencies Through Direct Assessment

Mastering CDA Competencies can help you earn your CDA Credential through Direct Assessment. Once you meet the basic eligibility requirements, *Mastering CDA Competencies* can boost your abilities in the six Competency Areas. You can read *Working with Young Children* and complete the coordinating chapters in *Mastering CDA Competencies* as a self-study project. The reading and practical exercises will prepare you to successfully complete your written assessment and interview by the Council representative. Once you complete the application process, the information obtained from *Mastering CDA Competencies* will help you succeed in the final requirements.

Using *Mastering CDA Competencies*

You will use *Mastering CDA Competencies* with the text *Working with Young Children*. Each chapter of this book corresponds to the same chapter in the text. The chapters begin by listing CDA Competency Goals and Functional Areas that the reading and exercises address. Each chapter of *Mastering CDA Competencies* is divided into the following four parts.

Part I: Read from *Working with Young Children*

Each reading assignment constitutes a complete chapter, and the 32 chapters combine to cover all CDA Competency Goals. Begin each assignment in *Mastering CDA Competencies* by reading the Competency Goals and Functional Areas the chapter covers, then read the coordinating chapter in your text.

Part II: Review What You Have Read

This section of *Mastering CDA Competencies* will help you review important concepts presented in the assigned textbook reading. It consists of short answer and essay questions to help you recall and review what you have read.

Part III: Observe What You Have Learned

Because observation is a key element in learning to work with children, this section will describe specific observations for you to do. Observations will become more advanced as you progress, until you ultimately plan, lead, and evaluate your own work with children. To help you, the section includes objectives, preparation instructions, setting details, and review questions that evaluate what you observe. Remember, this is designed to supplement text material. You must understand chapter concepts before conducting observation activities. The "Observing Children" section of this Introduction will explain how to observe children.

Part IV: Apply What You Have Learned

In the final section, you will implement what you've learned in reading assignments and observations. You may be asked to answer questions about situations you have observed, create your own teaching strategies, plan activities, or outline lessons. These activities will document your personal approach to early childhood education.

Self-Assessment

Before you begin any assignments, complete the "Pretraining Self-Assessment" found in this Introduction. These questions expand on the CDA Competency Goals and Functional Areas, and answering them will help you evaluate how well you perform the CDA skills at this point in your career. As you progress through the text and this book, try to implement what you learn during your work with young children. Return to this Introduction when you finish your fieldwork and complete the "Posttraining Self-Assessment" to track your professional growth.

Observing Children

Young children are fascinating to watch; just ask any new parent or proud grandparent! Children's attempts at trying new skills can be captivating, and observing them is something everyone enjoys.

Observation serves another purpose. It is one of the oldest methods of conducting research. Most information about child development has resulted from some form of observation; many times, children's behavior cannot be measured any other way. A one-year-old, for instance, can't answer questions verbally or in writing, but the child's behavior can speak for itself.

Professionals have used data gathered from formal observation to establish developmental norms. These norms include physical, cognitive, social, and emotional aspects of development as well as characteristics considered normal for children in specific age groups. These norms help teachers compare and note changes in the growth and development of children in their care. They will also help you as you observe young children and prepare for your child care career.

Forms of Observation

Early researchers recorded the behavior of each child in a diary, attempting to document every important event that occurred. Because this was very time-consuming, researchers later developed a variety of forms that made observations simpler and more precise. The three forms used in *Mastering CDA Competencies* are the narrative form, checklists, and rating scales. The type of form used depends upon what is being observed.

Narrative

The simplest form of observation is called *narrative,* during which the child's behavior is described in detail as it occurs. Once this process is completed, a second process, called *interpreting,* occurs after the observation takes place.

When using the narrative form of observation, your eyes act like a camera. You will record pictures of children playing, learning, and interacting. During your observation, you will record how children communicate verbally and nonverbally. You will record how they look and what they do. You'll note physical gestures, movements, and interactions with people and materials.

During the observation process, it is important to record only objective statements. To be objective, a statement must pass two tests. First, it must describe only observable actions. Therefore, do not include generalizations about children's motives, attitudes, and feelings. Secondly, the recorded information must be nonevaluative. It should not include why something happened or infer that what happened was wrong, right, good, or bad. Avoid labeling; do not infer any judgments or conclusions at this point. The following is an example of a narrative observation:

Sally arrived at the center holding her mother's hand. She slowing walked to her locker, removed her coat, and hung it in her locker. She turned to her mother and said, "You go to work." Sally's mother hugged her and said, "After work I'll take you to the dentist." Sally looked at her mother and started to cry.

She said, "I'm not going to the dentist. I'm staying here." Sally's mother reached out and hugged Sally. Sally continued crying and clung to her mother. The caregiver walked over to Sally and whispered in her ear. Then the caregiver put out her hand and said, "Come and look, Sally. We have a new friend at school today. Jodi brought her new hamster." Sally stopped crying and took the caregiver's hand. Together they walked to see the hamster. Sally's mother watched her for a moment, then left the room.

Notice only an objective description is recorded. The statements do not include causes, desires, emotions, explanations, feelings, goals, motives, purposes, needs, or wishes.

To help you learn to write an objective narrative, complete the following exercise. Then turn to the end of this introduction for the answers.

Objective Narrative Self-Test

Read each statement. Place a *D* in front of statements that are descriptive. Place an *I* in front of statements that are interpretive.

_____ 1. Jose opened the door and ran outside.

_____ 2. Mark left the blockbuilding area because he wasn't interested.

_____ 3. Mrs. Devery, the teacher, called each child's name.

_____ 4. When the burly was taken out of the box, the children were so excited they screamed.

_____ 5. The teacher said, "I like how quietly you are sitting."

_____ 6. The volunteer asked each child to name one color.

_____ 7. May cried because she could not speak English.

_____ 8. Kris hit Kelsi because she was in his way.

_____ 9. Wendy tipped over her glass of milk.

_____ 10. Maurice put the rabbit in the cage, shut the door, and closed the lock.

_____ 11. Tuanda walked across the room and sat next to Judy.

_____ 12. Sandy was confused by the teacher's directions, so she took another cookie.

Once the narrative data is recorded, a second process begins. This process involves interpreting the data, or attempting to explain the observed behavior and give it meaning. Why did the child behave as he or she did? What might have been the child's motivator? Did someone or something cause the child to act this way? Interpretation takes knowledge and skill. You should not attempt it without a thorough understanding of how children grow and develop. The observation itself serves no purpose without interpreting behavior and giving meaning to data.

Though an observation may be factual and unbiased, various interpretations are sometimes made. Since no two people are alike, no two people will interpret facts the same way. Each person who interprets a child's behavior may determine different motives for the behavior based on personal experiences. Their personal feelings, values, and attitudes may influence their interpretation of behavior.

To illustrate, an observer wrote the following:

Tony picked up the pitcher of milk. He moved the pitcher toward his glass. He hit the glass and tipped it over. The milk spilled.

When reviewing the observation of Tony, an observer might interpret his behavior in several ways:
- Tony was careless.
- Tony was inexperienced at handling a pitcher.
- Tony wasn't paying attention to what he was doing.
- Tony lacked the strength needed to lift the pitcher.
- Tony lacked the hand-eye coordination necessary to pour from the pitcher.

To decide which interpretation is most accurate, you would need to observe Tony on several occasions and over time. You would also need to understand thoroughly how children grow and develop.

Checklists

Another form of observation is called the *checklist*. Checklists are easy to use. They include specific behaviors to look for while observing a child or a group of children. The targeted behaviors are listed in a logical order, so you can record the presence or absence of a behavior quickly.

Rating Scales

Rating scales, the third form of observation, are used to record the degree to which a quality or trait is present. A checklist only indicates the presence or absence of a trait, but a rating scale tells how much or how little a trait is present.

Rating scales are easy to do and require little time to complete. Some rating scales contain only a numerical range; others define the behaviors more specifically. In order to decide on a rating, the observer should understand the behaviors he or she is rating.

Preparing to Observe

When assigned an observation activity from *Mastering CDA Competencies,* read through the entire activity. Study the objectives to determine the purpose of the observation. Note the behaviors for which you will be looking or the events you will be recording. It is important to know in advance what you'll be focusing on during the observation.

Each observation form in *Mastering CDA Competencies* follows a similar format. Record all information requested. On most of the forms, you will be asked to record the number of children present and their ages.

Guidelines for Observers

While studying young children, you will observe them in many situations. Whether in the play yard, in a classroom, or on a field trip, your behavior is important.

Whenever you gather data about children, you must use special care. **Keep the information you collect confidential.** This is perhaps the most important guideline to follow. Though you can discuss a child's behavior in your own classroom or seminar group, you must refrain from doing so outside that setting. Whenever you speak, remember other people are listening. The information you share could embarrass or even harm a child, parent, or teacher.

To protect confidentiality, your instructor or advisor may request you avoid using a child's name during classroom discussions. First names only are permitted in other classrooms. Both practices will help protect a child's identity. These practices will also prevent confidential information about a child from leaving the classroom.

Call the center to arrange an observation time. When you arrive at the center to observe, don't bring a coat, books, and other personal items into the classroom. Young children are especially curious about bags and purses, and these items may cause an unnecessary distraction or endanger the children's safety.

As you enter the class, be sensitive to what is happening in the room. Enter the room quietly. If the teacher is working with a group of children, avoid interrupting. Find a place to sit or stand, and wait for the teacher to approach you. If the children are involved in a self-selected play period, pause by the door until the teacher acknowledges your presence.

Indicate the length of time you will be present. Ask the teacher where he or she would like you to sit while you observe. This should be a place where you will not distract children.

During your observation, avoid talking with the children, other observers, or the staff. However, a child may ask what you are doing. If this happens, answer in a matter-of-fact manner. You might say you are watching the children play or writing notes on how children play.

Answers for Self-Test

1. D (Describes an observable behavior.)
2. I ("Because he wasn't interested" refers to an inferred motive.)
3. D
4. I ("We're so excited" is an inferred motive for screaming.)
5. D
6. D
7. I ("Because she could not speak English" is an inferred motive for crying.)
8. I ("Because she was in his way" is an inferred motive for hitting.)
9. D
10. D
11. D
12. I ("Was confused by the directions" is the inferred motive for taking another cookie.)

CDA Competency Goals and Functional Areas	Related Chapters in *Working with Young Children*
I. To establish and maintain a safe, healthy learning environment	Covered in chapters 8, 9, 10, 11, 12, 15, 16, 25, 28, 29, 30
1. **Safe:** Candidate provides a safe environment to prevent and reduce injuries.	Covered in chapters 10, 11, 15, 27, 28
2. **Healthy:** Candidate promotes good health and nutrition and provides an environment that contributes to the prevention of illness.	Covered in chapters 10, 11, 12, 16, 25, 28
3. **Learning Environment:** Candidate uses space, relationships, materials, and routines as resources for constructing an interesting, secure, and enjoyable environment that encourages play, exploration, and learning.	Covered in chapters 8, 9, 10, 11, 16, 28, 29, 30
II. To advance physical and intellectual competence	Covered in chapters 19, 20, 21, 22, 23, 24, 26, 27, 28, 29
4. **Physical:** Candidate provides a variety of equipment, activities, and opportunities to promote the physical development of children.	Covered in chapters 3, 4, 5, 6, 7, 16, 17, 18, 19, 20, 21, 26, 27, 28
5. **Cognitive:** Candidate provides activities and opportunities that encourage curiosity, exploration, and problem solving appropriate to the developmental levels and learning styles of children.	Covered in chapters 3, 4, 5, 6, 7, 16, 17, 18, 19, 20, 21, 22, 23, 24, 25, 26, 27, 28, 29
6. **Communication:** Candidate actively communicates with children and provides opportunities and support for children to understand, acquire, and use verbal and nonverbal means of communicating thoughts and feelings.	Covered in chapters 13, 14, 17, 18, 19, 20, 21, 23, 24, 25, 26, 27, 28, 29
7. **Creative:** Candidate provides opportunities that stimulate children to play with sound, rhythm, language, materials, space, and ideas in individual ways and to express their creative abilities.	Covered in chapters 17, 18, 19, 20, 26, 28, 29
III. To support social and emotional development and provide positive guidance	Covered in chapters 4, 5, 6, 7, 14, 16, 28, 29
8. **Self:** Candidate provides physical and emotional security for each child and helps each child to know, accept, and take pride in himself or herself and to develop a sense of independence.	Covered in chapters 1, 3, 13, 15, 24, 28, 29
9. **Social:** Candidate helps each child feel accepted in the group, helps children learn to communicate and get along with others, and encourages feelings of empathy and mutual respect among children and adults.	Covered in chapters 3, 4, 5, 6, 7, 13, 15, 17, 24, 27, 28, 29
10. **Guidance:** Candidate provides a supportive environment in which children can begin to learn and practice appropriate and acceptable behaviors as individuals and as a group.	Covered in chapters 3, 7, 8, 13, 14, 15, 16, 28, 29
IV. To establish positive and productive relationships with families	Covered in chapters 25, 31
11. **Families:** Candidate maintains an open, friendly, and cooperative relationship with each child's family; encourages their involvement in the program; and supports the child's relationship with his or her family.	Covered in chapters 25, 31

CDA Competency Goals and Functional Areas	Related Chapters in *Working with Young Children*
V. To ensure a well-run, purposeful program responsive to participant needs	Covered in chapters 1, 3, 17, 28, 29
12. **Program Management:** Candidate is a manager who uses all available resources to ensure an effective operation. The Candidate is a competent organizer, planner, record keeper, communicator, and a cooperative coworker.	Covered in chapters 1, 3, 17, 28
VI. To maintain a commitment to professionalism	Covered in chapters 1, 2, 32
13. **Professionalism:** Candidate makes decisions based on knowledge of early childhood theories and practices; promotes quality in child care services; and takes advantage of opportunities to improve competence, both for personal and professional growth and for the benefit of children and families.	Covered in chapters 1, 2, 32

Copyright Goodheart-Willcox Co., Inc.

	Pretraining Self-Assessment			Posttraining Self-Assessment		
COMPETENCY GOAL I: **To establish and maintain a safe, healthy learning environment**	Regularly	Sometimes	Never	Regularly	Sometimes	Never
1. Functional Area: Safe						
I keep both the inside of the center and the outdoor play area free of debris; structural hazards; unguarded space heaters; tools; and dangerous substances, such as medicine, cleaning products, matches, chipped paint, toxic plants, small objects, balloons, and plastic bags.						
I ensure that safety equipment, such as fire extinguishers and smoke detectors, is in place and operable and that someone knows how to use it.						
I maintain a current list of phone numbers for contacting parents and emergency services, such as poison control, fire company, and medical help.						
I use diagrams, pictures, and words that are easy for children and adults to understand. I post instructions and practice emergency procedures, including safety procedures for disabled children.						
I plan and practice monthly fire drills with children in my care.						
I check daily that outdoor equipment is safe for children and is in good repair.						
I respond immediately and sympathetically to a child's injury or fear of injury, and I encourage the same response by the children.						
I take safety precautions in a reassuring manner without overprotecting or making children fearful.						
I anticipate and plan to prevent potentially dangerous situations, such as leaving sleeping children unattended.						
I maintain first aid supplies—gauze, tape, syrup of ipecac, tweezers, scissors, and soap—and know basic first aid procedures appropriate for young children, such as how to handle choking and treat cuts.						
I use safe auto and bus travel procedures, including appropriate car seats for children.						
I discuss safety information with parents and tell them about resources, such as poison control centers.						
I supervise all children's indoor and outdoor activities.						
I know current information about safety standards for toys and equipment and share this information with parents and the center staff.						
I adapt the indoor and outdoor environments to enhance disabled children's independence.						
I require written parental authorization before allowing people other than parents to pick up children from the center.						
2. Functional Area: Healthy						
I conduct activities in a positive, relaxed, and pleasant atmosphere to reduce tension and stress.						
I wash my hands before and after helping children toilet, blow their noses, and before preparing food and eating.						
I attend to each child's physical needs, such as toileting, eating, exercising, and napping.						
I provide affection to all children.						

(Continued)

Copyright Goodheart-Willcox Co., Inc.

	Pretraining Self-Assessment			Posttraining Self-Assessment		
COMPETENCY GOAL I: *(Continued)* **To establish and maintain a safe, healthy learning environment**	*Regularly*	*Sometimes*	*Never*	*Regularly*	*Sometimes*	*Never*
2. Functional Area: Healthy *(Continued)*						
I provide adequate ventilation and lighting, comfortable room temperatures, and good sanitation.						
I clean play areas and materials daily.						
I have established procedures for the care of sick children, such as isolating a child with a contagious illness from well children, contacting parents and medical providers, and administering medicine.						
I help children develop basic health habits.						
I keep current emergency telephone numbers for each child's parent(s) or guardian(s), nearest relative, and medical providers.						
I communicate frequently with parents about children's health, nutrition, communicable diseases, and medications.						
I follow center procedures for maintaining health records and administering medications and first aid.						
I establish a relaxed mealtime routine that makes eating pleasant for each child.						
I inform parents about health resources, such as physicians or community clinics with family services.						
I recognize unusual behaviors and physical symptoms in children and encourage parents to obtain appropriate treatment.						
I work cooperatively with health professionals and parents to meet children's needs.						
I recognize the signs of health crises, such as seizures, that children with special needs may have, and I respond appropriately.						
I recognize symptoms of possible abuse and neglect and am aware of play or behavior that indicates physical or sexual abuse.						
3. Functional Area: Learning Environment						
I use materials, books, and equipment that stimulate children and suit individual learning styles.						
I use materials that demonstrate acceptance of each child's sex, family, race, language, and culture.						
I provide easily accessible learning materials, such as puzzles, books, and stacking toys, that children can explore independently. I also reserve some materials for special occasions.						
I organize space into identifiable areas that encourage appropriate and independent use of materials.						
I balance active and quiet, free and unstructured, individual and group, and indoor and outdoor activities.						
I provide opportunities for children to develop their senses and concentration skills.						
I provide a variety of natural and pleasurable sounds, such as music, normal conversation, and outdoor sounds.						
I frequently observe individual children as well as the group and modify the environment to meet changing abilities, needs, and interests.						

(Continued)

Copyright Goodheart-Willcox Co., Inc.

	Pretraining Self-Assessment			Posttraining Self-Assessment		
COMPETENCY GOAL I: *(Continued)* **To establish and maintain a safe, healthy learning environment**	Regularly	Sometimes	Never	Regularly	Sometimes	Never
3. Functional Area: Learning Environment *(Continued)*						
I vary routines to take advantage of unusual opportunities, such as going outside in the snow or watching workers on the street.						
I support relationships between adults and children and among children in my care as an important aspect of the learning environment.						
I schedule the day so each child receives individual attention.						
I provide activities that extend children's attention spans.						
I provide simple and consistent routines for mealtimes, naps, transitions, and cleanup, and I support children's learning through these routines.						
I adapt the daily schedule to accommodate children with special needs rather than requiring them to fit the schedule.						
I seek information about sexual abuse, child abuse, and neglect; keep current on laws and policies concerning reporting and treating abuse; and learn how to work with affected children and families.						
COMPETENCY GOAL II: To advance physical and intellectual competence						
4. Functional Area: Physical						
I arrange and encourage physical activities according to how children's physical development affects their cognitive, social, and emotional development.						
I observe and evaluate children's developmental abilities and provide activities at levels appropriate for each child.						
I plan and participate daily in appropriate large-muscle activities, such as playing ball, running, and jumping.						
I provide a variety of activities from children's cultures, such as dances, music, fingerplays, and active games.						
I provide opportunities for children to develop their senses by noticing colors, smelling odors, distinguishing sounds, feeling and touching various objects, and tasting different foods.						
I communicate to children and their parents the importance of outdoor play and physical activity for healthy growth and development.						
I plan for and support children's changing needs for active play, quiet activity, and rest.						
I encourage but never force children who fear physical activity because of illness, accidents, abuse, limited opportunity, or overprotective caregivers and parents.						
I observe and evaluate children's physical development, recognize signs of possible physical disabilities and developmental lags, refer parents to appropriate services, and follow up on referrals or individual development plans.						
I adapt the program to meet the special needs of children with disabilities, realizing how physical development influences self-concept and social development.						

(Continued)

Copyright Goodheart-Willcox Co., Inc.

	Pretraining Self-Assessment			Posttraining Self-Assessment		
COMPETENCY GOAL II: *(Continued)* **To advance physical and intellectual competence**	Regularly	Sometimes	Never	Regularly	Sometimes	Never
4. Functional Area: Physical *(Continued)*						
I avoid overprotecting children with disabilities, support their independence, include them in physical activities with other children, and modify activities when necessary. I also encourage parents to do the same.						
5. Functional Area: Cognitive						
I observe children during play to assess their cognitive development and readiness for new learning opportunities.						
I use techniques and activities that stimulate children's curiosity, inventiveness, problem-solving abilities, and communication skills.						
I give children time and space for extended concentrated play, and I adjust routines and schedules for this purpose.						
I provide opportunities for children to experiment with the relationships of cause and effect and means and ends.						
I understand the importance of play and often join children's play activities as a partner and facilitator.						
I use the center environment, everyday activities, and homemade materials to encourage children's intellectual development.						
I help children discover ways to solve problems that arise in daily activities.						
I support children's repetitions of the familiar and introduce new experiences, activities, and materials when they are interested and ready.						
I recognize differences in individual learning styles and find ways to work effectively with each child.						
I encourage children to learn actively rather than promote an atmosphere in which adults talk and children listen passively.						
I obtain (or make) and use special learning materials and equipment for children whose disabilities affect their abilities to learn.						
I provide equipment and materials that children can explore and master independently.						
I am aware of the task a child is attempting and provide appropriate support.						
I recognize learning problems and make referrals according to the center's policy.						
6. Functional Area: Communication						
I have realistic expectations for each child's understanding and use of speech that are based on my knowledge of language development and the child.						
I frequently talk with children individually and stimulate conversation among children as well as between children and adults in the room.						
I provide activities that encourage children to develop listening and comprehension skills.						
I help children connect word meaning(s) to experiences and real objects.						

(Continued)

Copyright Goodheart-Willcox Co., Inc.

COMPETENCY GOAL II: *(Continued)* **To advance physical and intellectual competence**	Pretraining Self-Assessment			Posttraining Self-Assessment		
	Regularly	Sometimes	Never	Regularly	Sometimes	Never
6. Functional Area: Communication *(Continued)*						
I recognize, understand, and respect local speech patterns and idioms.						
I respect the language of non-English-speaking families, encourage them to communicate freely with their children in the language parents prefer, and help them find opportunities to learn English.						
I am aware of the caregiver's role as a language model for children and use affectionate and playful tones, clear speech, and responsive conversation.						
I listen attentively to children, try to understand what they want to communicate, and help them express themselves.						
I share children's communication/language achievements with parents.						
I use a variety of songs, stories, books, and games including those from children's cultures—for language development.						
I talk with children about special relationships and experiences in their families and at home.						
I recognize possible impairments or delays that affect hearing and speech and help families find resources, cooperate with treatment plans, and find ways to communicate positively with these children.						
7. Functional Area: Creative						
I realize the process of creating is as important and sometimes more important than the product.						
I understand that each child's creative expression is unique and do not encourage uniformity.						
I allow time for spontaneous and extended play within the daily routine.						
I include a variety of music, art, literature, dance, role playing, celebrations, and other creative activities from the children's cultures in program activities.						
I participate in make-believe games with children.						
I model and encourage children's creativity in language through rhymes, imaginative stories, and nonsense words.						
I provide unstructured materials such as blocks, paint, clay, or musical instruments that are appropriate for various developmental levels.						
I encourage thorough, repeated exploration of creative materials whenever possible, such as leaving a block structure standing so that building can continue the next day or allowing one child to play in the sensory table for an extended period of time.						
I model creativity by using homemade materials and found objects.						
I help parents understand the importance of creative expression in child development and the need to provide children with opportunities for creative activities, such as storytelling and using art materials.						
I encourage children to try new and different activities.						

(Continued)

Copyright Goodheart-Willcox Co., Inc.

	Pretraining Self-Assessment			Posttraining Self-Assessment		
COMPETENCY GOAL II: *(Continued)* **To advance physical and intellectual competence**	Regularly	Sometimes	Never	Regularly	Sometimes	Never
7. Functional Area: Creative *(Continued)*						
I provide opportunities for "messy activities", such as water and sand play, finger painting, and drawing with markers.						
COMPETENCY GOAL III: **To support social and emotional development and provide positive guidance**						
8. Functional Area: Self						
I treat each child as an individual with his or her own strengths, needs, and unique characteristics.						
I am sensitive to different cultural values and expectations concerning independence and expression of feelings.						
I address each child by name, talk with each child daily, and encourage each child to call other children and adults by name.						
I have affectionate and appropriate physical contact with each child daily in ways that convey love, affection, and security.						
I help children through periods of stress, separation, transition, and other crises.						
I offer children choices in activities, materials, and foods when possible, and I respect their choices.						
I encourage and help children to practice skills when eating, getting dressed, using toys and equipment, cleaning up, and helping others.						
I give one-on-one attention to each child as often as possible.						
I enjoy children and express this enjoyment to them directly.						
I delight in each child's success, express kindness and support when a child is having trouble, and help him or her learn from mistakes.						
I help children recognize, label, and accept their feelings and express them in culturally appropriate ways.						
I model recognition and expression of feelings by naming my feelings as I express them.						
I provide many opportunities for all children, including those with disabilities, to feel effective, experience success, and gain the positive recognition of others.						
I understand the effects of abuse and neglect on children's self-concepts and work sensitively with these children.						
9. Functional Area: Social						
I understand the stages of social development and help children and parents deal with issues of separation anxiety, negative behavior, shyness, sexual identity, and friendship.						
I have realistic expectations for young children's social behavior based on their levels of development.						
I serve as a social model by building a positive relationship with each child and parent and by maintaining positive relationships with other adults in the center.						

(Continued)

Copyright Goodheart-Willcox Co., Inc.

COMPETENCY GOAL III: *(Continued)* **To support social and emotional development and provide positive guidance**	Pretraining Self-Assessment			Posttraining Self-Assessment		
	Regularly	Sometimes	Never	Regularly	Sometimes	Never
9. Functional Area: Social *(Continued)*						
I respond quickly and calmly to prevent children from hurting themselves and each other.						
I help children learn to respect the rights and possessions of others.						
I encourage children to ask for, accept, and give help to each other.						
I encourage children to make friends.						
I help children become aware of their feelings and those of others by encouraging them to discuss feelings with each other.						
I encourage children to express their feelings and assert their rights in socially acceptable ways.						
I encourage play and relationships among children across racial, language, ethnic, age, gender, and ability groupings.						
10. Functional Area: Guidance						
I know a variety of techniques for positive guidance and use them appropriately.						
I relate guidance practices to knowledge of each child's personality and level of development.						
I avoid negative methods such as spanking, shouting, threatening, or shaming.						
I establish guidelines for children's behavior that are simple, reasonable, and consistent to encourage self-control.						
I establish routines that are consistent and reliable yet flexible to children's needs.						
I alert children to changes in activities or routines well in advance and handle transitions from one activity to another with clear directions and patience.						
I modify play when children become overstimulated.						
I build a trusting relationship with children as a foundation for positive guidance and self-discipline.						
I anticipate confrontations among children and defuse provocative behavior.						
I address a problem behavior or situation rather than label the child involved.						
I accept children's sad or angry feelings, provide acceptable outlets for children to express them, and teach feeling words.						
I help parents develop realistic expectations for children's behavior in ways that help avoid disciplinary problems.						
I encourage parents to talk about child-rearing techniques, guidance, and self-discipline and refer them to classes, books, and other resources as appropriate.						
I know parents' discipline methods and expectations and select those appropriate for the center.						

(Continued)

Copyright Goodheart-Willcox Co., Inc.

	Pretraining Self-Assessment			Posttraining Self-Assessment		
COMPETENCY GOAL III: *(Continued)* **To support social and emotional development and provide positive guidance**	Regularly	Sometimes	Never	Regularly	Sometimes	Never
10. Functional Area: Guidance *(Continued)*						
I understand that sometimes serious behavior problems are related to developmental or emotional problems, and I work cooperatively with parents toward solutions.						
I am aware of each child's limitations and abilities, use guidance techniques accordingly, and explain rules at the child's level of understanding.						
COMPETENCY GOAL IV: **To establish positive and productive relationships with families**						
11. Functional Area: Families						
I recognize that children's primary caregivers may be single mothers or fathers, both parents, stepparents, grandparents, uncles, aunts, sisters, brothers, foster parents, or guardians.						
I help parents understand child development as well as the child's point of view.						
I provide opportunities for parents and other family members to share their skills and talents in the program.						
I recognize that caregivers can support parents in their role.						
I offer parents information about health and social services and other community resources.						
I respect each family's cultural background, religious beliefs, and child-rearing practices.						
I observe strict confidentiality regarding children and families and make parents aware of this policy.						
I suggest activities and materials that parents can share with children at home.						
I am able to discuss problem behavior with parents in a constructive, supportive manner.						
I support parents in making arrangements for school or an alternative child care program when necessary.						
I become attached to children without competing with parents.						
I encourage parents to visit the center, participate in activities, and make suggestions for the daily program.						
I respect and try to understand the parents' views when they differ from the program's goals or policies and attempt to resolve the differences.						
I tell parents about children's achievements and share their pleasure in new abilities.						
I help parents separate from children, recognizing parents' possible concerns about leaving them.						
I support children and families under stress, working cooperatively with other professionals as appropriate.						
I help parents recognize their feelings and attitudes about conditions for disabled children.						
I help parents identify resources to diagnose and treat disabled children.						
I help parents obtain clear information about their children's special needs and the family's legal right to services.						

(Continued)

Copyright Goodheart-Willcox Co., Inc.

	Pretraining Self-Assessment			Posttraining Self-Assessment		
COMPETENCY GOAL IV: *(Continued)* **To establish positive and productive relationships with families**	Regularly	Sometimes	Never	Regularly	Sometimes	Never
11. Functional Area: Families *(Continued)*						
I encourage parents to communicate confidently about their children with government and other community agencies and help them to do so.						
COMPETENCY GOAL V: **To ensure a well-run, purposeful program responsive to participant needs**						
12. Functional Area: Program Management						
I work with parents to identify the strengths and needs of each child.						
I develop skills in observing and recording information about children and their families in a nonjudgmental manner, and I use the information to plan and implement the daily program.						
I maintain up-to-date records concerning the growth, health, behavior, and progress of each child as well as the group. I share this information with parents and center personnel.						
I consider goals and objectives for each child as well as the group and develop realistic plans that are responsive to children's needs.						
I implement plans for each child by identifying developmentally and culturally appropriate activities and materials for each day.						
I clearly understand my responsibilities within the program.						
I discuss issues that affect the program with staff and follow up on their resolutions.						
I work as a team member with classroom staff as well as substitutes, parents, and volunteers.						
I support other staff by offering assistance and supervision when needed.						
I make or obtain materials and equipment appropriate for children's developmental needs.						
I work with staff to choose substitutes carefully, requiring experience with children of the same ages whenever possible.						
I orient new or substitute caregivers and volunteers to the routines, special needs, and abilities of each child.						
I implement procedures to help children make smooth transitions from one group to another.						
I know community social service, health, and education resources and use them when appropriate.						
I recognize developmental problems, work with parents and specialists to develop plans specific to meet each child's needs, implement recommended treatment by following up on referrals, and work with the family to meet goals for the child.						
I establish communication with community services that respond to family violence.						

(Continued)

Copyright Goodheart-Willcox Co., Inc.

	Pretraining Self-Assessment			Posttraining Self-Assessment		
COMPETENCY GOAL VI: To maintain a commitment to professionalism	Regularly	Sometimes	Never	Regularly	Sometimes	Never
13. Functional Area: Professionalism						
I enjoy working with young children in a group setting and present a positive attitude.						
I understand the program's philosophy and can describe its goals and objectives to others.						
I continue to gain knowledge of physical, cognitive, language, emotional, and social development in order to plan program goals.						
I keep all personal information about children and families confidential.						
I continually evaluate my own performance and strive to grow professionally.						
I participate in peer evaluation and am able to accept comments and criticism from colleagues, supervisors, and parents in a constructive manner.						
I take advantage of opportunities for professional and personal development by joining appropriate professional organizations and attending meetings, training courses, and conferences.						
I am informed about current child care practices, research, legislation, and other developments in early childhood education.						
I advocate quality services and rights for children and families.						
I work cooperatively with other staff members, accept supervision, and help promote a positive atmosphere in the center.						
I learn about new laws and regulations affecting center care, children, and families.						
I work with other professionals and parents to develop effective strategies to communicate the needs of children and families to decision makers.						
I request additional resources for individual children and the program.						
I recognize that special skills are necessary to work effectively with children at different ages and developmental stages, and I seek appropriate information and training.						
I am aware that some normal developmental characteristics of children, such as crying, dependency, willfulness, and negative behavior, often make adults feel uncomfortable. I acknowledge these feelings in myself, coworkers, and parents while minimizing negative reactions toward children.						

Copyright Goodheart-Willcox Co., Inc.

You: Working with Young Children

■ Competency Goals:

■ To ensure a well-run, purposeful program responsive to participant needs
■ To maintain a commitment to professionalism

■ Functional Areas:

■ Self
■ Program Management
■ Professionalism

Part I: Read from *Working with Young Children*

■ Chapter 1

Part II: Review What You Have Read

Directions: Answer the following questions.

1. What age span constitutes early childhood? _____

2. Why will the need for child care professionals continue to grow? _____

   _____

   _____

   _____

   _____

   _____

3. Describe the role of licensing specialists. _____

   _____

   _____

   _____

   _____

   _____

   _____

4. Why is it important to understand how children grow and develop? _____

   _____

   _____

   _____

   _____

   _____

(Continued)

Copyright Goodheart-Willcox Co., Inc.

5. On what four areas do developmentally appropriate curricula focus? _____

_____

_____

_____

6. How does the environment affect children's development? _____

_____

_____

_____

_____

_____

7. Why is it essential for child care professionals to communicate effectively? _____

_____

_____

_____

_____

8. What is the primary professional organization for teachers of young children? _____

_____

9. Why is it important to respect all children in your care? _____

_____

_____

_____

_____

_____

10. Why is a sense of humor helpful when working with children? _____

_____

_____

_____

_____

_____

_____

Copyright Goodheart-Willcox Co., Inc.

Part III: Observe What You Have Learned

Teacher Responsibilities

■ Objectives

After completing this activity, you will be able to
- ■ identify the responsibilities of a child care professional
- ■ describe how responsibilities vary in the amount of time they require and according to children's ages
- ■ identify and accentuate your positive traits when working with children
- ■ identify and strengthen areas needing improvement

■ Preparation

1. Arrange to spend a minimum of one hour observing a child care teacher, teacher's aide, director, or kindergarten teacher. Call ahead to schedule the observation.

2. Study the responsibilities outlined in the text for the position of the person you choose to observe.

■ Setting

Place where observation occurred _____

_____

Phone number _____

Time _____ to _____

Name of person observed _____

Title

Date

Number of children present _____

Ages of children _____

■ The Observation

Observe a child care professional for a minimum of one hour. Record his or her responsibilities.

Time	Responsibilities

(Continued)

Copyright Goodheart-Willcox Co., Inc.

Observe What You Have Learned (Cont.)

Time	Responsibilities

■ Review What You Have Observed

1. What responsibilities required the most time? _____

_____

_____

_____

2. How much time did the teacher spend maintaining equipment? _____

_____

_____

_____

3. How did responsibilities vary depending on the time of day or the children's ages? _____

_____

_____

_____

4. Did the teacher alter curriculum to meet children's immediate needs? Explain. _____

_____

_____

_____

5. How did the caregiver help each child feel important, respected, and valued? Explain. _____

_____

_____

_____

_____

Copyright Goodheart-Willcox Co., Inc.

Part IV: Apply What You Have Learned

1. People who enjoy working with young children tend to share some of the characteristics listed below. For each characteristic, rate yourself as (S) strong, (A) average, or (W) weak. After rating yourself, ask a colleague, family member, or friend to rate you using the same rating sheet.

_____ active	_____ energetic	_____ practical
_____ affectionate	_____ enthusiastic	_____ realistic
_____ alert	_____ firm	_____ resourceful
_____ ambitious	_____ flexible	_____ responsible
_____ artistic	_____ friendly	_____ self-controlled
_____ broad-minded	_____ healthy	_____ sensible
_____ calm	_____ honest	_____ serious
_____ capable	_____ humorous	_____ sincere
_____ careful	_____ intelligent	_____ stable
_____ competent	_____ kind	_____ thorough
_____ considerate	_____ levelheaded	_____ tolerant
_____ cooperative	_____ likable	_____ understanding
_____ creative	_____ nurturing	_____ warm
_____ dependable	_____ organized	_____ well-groomed
_____ eager	_____ patient	_____ wholesome
_____ efficient	_____ positive	

2. List additional characteristics describing people who work with young children. Rate yourself in these areas, too.

_____

_____

_____

_____

_____

_____

_____

_____

_____

_____

_____

_____

(Continued)

Copyright Goodheart-Willcox Co., Inc.

3. Ask a colleague, family member, or friend to rate you for each characteristic as (S) strong, (A) average, or (W) weak.

_____ active	_____ energetic	_____ practical
_____ affectionate	_____ enthusiastic	_____ realistic
_____ alert	_____ firm	_____ resourceful
_____ ambitious	_____ flexible	_____ responsible
_____ artistic	_____ friendly	_____ self-controlled
_____ broad-minded	_____ healthy	_____ sensible
_____ calm	_____ honest	_____ serious
_____ capable	_____ humorous	_____ sincere
_____ careful	_____ intelligent	_____ stable
_____ competent	_____ kind	_____ thorough
_____ considerate	_____ levelheaded	_____ tolerant
_____ cooperative	_____ likable	_____ understanding
_____ creative	_____ nurturing	_____ warm
_____ dependable	_____ organized	_____ well-groomed
_____ eager	_____ patient	_____ wholesome
_____ efficient	_____ positive	

4. How will your strengths benefit you in an early childhood career?

_____
_____
_____
_____
_____
_____

5. What actions can you take to strengthen your weak areas?

_____
_____
_____
_____
_____
_____
_____
_____

Copyright Goodheart-Willcox Co., Inc.

Types of Early Childhood Programs

■ Competency Goal:

■ To maintain a commitment to professionalism

■ Functional Area:

■ Professionalism

Part I: Read from *Working with Young Children*

■ Chapter 2

Part II: Review What You Have Read

Directions: Answer the following questions.

1. What is the most common type of child care in the United States?_____
   _____

2. What is the focus of most child care centers? _____
   _____
   _____
   _____

3. Describe the teacher's role in a Montessori school. _____
   _____
   _____
   _____

4. Why is nutrition a vital part of the Head Start program? _____
   _____
   _____
   _____
   _____
   _____

5. List the three basic scheduling patterns in kindergarten. _____
   _____
   _____
   _____

(Continued)

6. Compare the advantages and disadvantages of parent cooperatives. _____

_____

_____

_____

_____

_____

_____

7. Describe the differences between publicly sponsored programs and privately sponsored programs. _____

_____

_____

_____

_____

_____

_____

8. Describe a chain child care center. _____

_____

_____

_____

_____

_____

9. List one advantage and disadvantage of company-owned, on-site child care._____

_____

_____

_____

_____

10. What factors influence selection of a child care program?_____

_____

_____

_____

_____

_____

_____

Copyright Goodheart-Willcox Co., Inc.

Part III: Observe What You Have Learned

■ Selecting Child Care

■ Objectives

After completing this activity, you will be able to
■ evaluate an early childhood program
■ identify your feelings about the child care program

■ Preparation

1. Arrange an appointment with a child care director to discuss the program and observe the facility.
2. Review the questions on the chart below.

■ Setting

Place where observation occurred _____

_____

Name of caregiver_____

Caregiver's education _____

Teaching experience _____

Length of time in center _____

Staff size _____

Number of programs _____

Number of children enrolled _____

■ The Observation

As you talk with the director and tour the center, complete the chart that follows.

	Yes	No
Is the center accredited by the National Academy of Early Childhood Programs?		
Do the children appear to be happy, active, and secure?		
Are all staff members educationally qualified?		
Do staff members attend in-service trainings, professional meetings, and conferences on a regular basis?		
Are staff meetings conducted regularly to plan and evaluate program activities?		
Do staff members observe, assess, and record each child's developmental progress?		
Does the curriculum support the children's individual rates of development?		
Do the staff and curriculum celebrate diversity?		
Is the indoor and outdoor environment large enough to support a variety of activities?		
Is the environment inviting, warm, and stimulating?		

(Continued)

Copyright Goodheart-Willcox Co., Inc.

Observe What You Have Learned (Cont.)

	Yes	No
Is equipment provided to promote all four areas of development: physical, cognitive, social, and emotional?		
Are safe and sanitary conditions maintained within the building and on the play yard?		
Are teacher-child interactions positive?		
Are teachers using developmentally appropriate teaching strategies?		
Are parents welcome to observe and participate?		
Is sufficient equipment provided for the number of children attending?		
Does the climate in the center "feel" positive?		
Do teachers meet with parents regularly to discuss the child's needs, interests, and abilities?		

■ Review What You Have Observed

1. What three questions indicate the program's greatest strengths? _____

_____

_____

_____

2. What three questions indicate the program's greatest weaknesses? _____

_____

_____

_____

3. As a parent, would you send your child to this center? Explain your answer. _____

_____

_____

_____

_____

_____

_____

4. As a caregiver, would you want to work at this center? Why or why not? _____

_____

_____

_____

_____

_____

_____

Copyright Goodheart-Willcox Co., Inc.

Part IV: Apply What You Have Learned

1. Pretend you are a parent seeking an early childhood program for your child. Visit two centers and evaluate them by checking the appropriate answers to the questions below. Then summarize your overall impressions of each program, describing which you would choose for your child and why.

Name of center #1 _____

Name of center #2 _____

	Center #1		Center #2	
	Yes	No	Yes	No
Is the center accredited by the National Academy of Early Childhood Programs?				
Do the children appear to be happy, active, and secure?				
Are all staff members educationally qualified?				
Do staff members attend in-service trainings, professional meetings, and conferences on a regular basis?				
Are staff meetings conducted regularly to plan and evaluate program activities?				
Do staff members observe, assess, and record each child's developmental progress?				
Does the curriculum support the children's individual rates of development?				
Do the staff and curriculum celebrate diversity?				
Is the indoor and outdoor environment large enough to support a variety of activities?				
Is the environment inviting, warm, and stimulating?				
Is equipment provided to promote all four areas of development: physical, cognitive, social, and emotional?				
Are safe and sanitary conditions maintained within the building and on the play yard?				
Are teacher-child interactions positive?				
Are teachers using developmentally appropriate teaching strategies?				
Are parents welcome to observe and participate?				
Is sufficient equipment provided for the number of children attending?				
Does the climate in the center "feel" positive?				
Do teachers meet with parents regularly to discuss the child's needs, interests, and abilities?				

(Continued)

Copyright Goodheart-Willcox Co., Inc.

Apply What You Have Learned (Cont.)

2. Evaluate center #1 _____

_____

_____

_____

_____

_____

_____

_____

_____

3. Evaluate center #2 _____

_____

_____

_____

_____

_____

_____

_____

_____

4. Which center would you choose? Why? _____

_____

_____

_____

_____

_____

_____

_____

_____

Copyright Goodheart-Willcox Co., Inc.

Observing Children: A Tool for Assessment

■ Competency Goals:

- ■ To advance physical and intellectual competence
- ■ To support social and emotional development and provide positive guidance
- ■ To ensure a well-run program responsive to participant needs

■ Functional Areas:

- ■ Physical
- ■ Cognitive
- ■ Social
- ■ Self
- ■ Program Management
- ■ Guidance

Part I: Read from *Working with Young Children*

- ■ Chapter 3

Part II: Review What You Have Read

Directions: Answer the following questions.

1. Why is observation important? _____

   _____

   _____

2. Distinguish between assessment and observation. _____

   _____

   _____

   _____

   _____

3. What are the purposes of assessment? _____

   _____

   _____

   _____

   _____

4. What is the difference between initial assessment and ongoing assessment? _____

   _____

   _____

   _____

   _____

(Continued)

Copyright Goodheart-Willcox Co., Inc.

5. What are the three considerations for choosing a method of assessment?_____
_____
_____
_____

6. Describe the two tests to make sure an anecdotal record is objective._____
_____
_____
_____
_____

7. What are the advantages and disadvantages of checklists? _____
_____
_____
_____
_____
_____

8. Why are rating scales used by teachers?_____
_____
_____
_____
_____

9. What can be included in a child's portfolio?_____
_____
_____
_____
_____
_____
_____

10. List three guidelines to use when observing children. _____
_____
_____
_____

Copyright Goodheart-Willcox Co., Inc.

Part III: Observe What You Have Learned

■ Writing Anecdotal Records

■ Objectives

After completing this activity, you will be able to
- write an anecdotal record
- evaluate an anecdotal record for its objectivity

■ Preparation

1. Arrange to observe a child in a preschool, child care center, or Head Start Center.

2. Review the content of an anecdotal record.

■ Setting

Place where observation occurred _____

_____

Address _____

Phone number _____

Contact person _____

Date _____Time _____ to _____

Name of child _____ Birthdate_____

Other information _____

_____

_____

_____

■ The Observation

Review the contents of an anecdotal record. Observe a child and record an incident on the form provided. Finally, evaluate your anecdotal record.

■ Contents of anecdotal records:
- Identify the child and the child's age.
- Include the date, time of day, and setting.
- Identify the observer.
- Provide an accurate account of the child's actions and conversations.
- Include responses of other children and/or adults, if they are involved in the situation.

Anecdotal Record

Child's Name: _____ Date: _____

Child's Age: _____ Years _____ Months _____

Setting: _____ Time: _____ to _____

Observer: _____

Incident: _____

_____

_____

_____

_____

_____

_____

_____

_____

_____

_____

_____

_____

_____

_____

_____

_____

_____

_____

_____

_____

_____

_____

Copyright Goodheart-Willcox Co., Inc.

■ Review What You Have Observed

1. Review your anecdotal record. Does it include who was involved, what happened, when it happened, and where it occurred? Explain. _____

_____

_____

_____

_____

_____

2. Did your record include how the children communicated verbally and nonverbally? Explain. _____

_____

_____

_____

_____

_____

3. Was all the recorded information observable? Explain. _____

_____

_____

_____

_____

_____

4. Was the recorded information nonevaluative? Explain. _____

_____

_____

_____

_____

5. Was only an objective description of the observed behavior recorded? Did your statements include any of the following: causes, emotions, feelings, goals, motives, desires, purposes, needs, or wishes? _____

_____

_____

_____

_____

(Continued)

Copyright Goodheart-Willcox Co., Inc.

6. Why is it important to keep your observations objective? _____

_____

_____

_____

_____

Part IV: Apply What You Have Learned

1. What is the final purpose for assessment? _____

_____

_____

_____

2. Describe the assessment methods used in your center. _____

_____

_____

_____

_____

_____

3. How could you improve the assessment process in your center? _____

_____

_____

_____

_____

_____

_____

4. A portfolio is a collection of materials that shows a person's abilities, accomplishments, and progress over time. List materials that could be included in a child's portfolio. _____

_____

_____

_____

_____

Copyright Goodheart-Willcox Co., Inc.

Understanding Children from Birth to Age Two

■ Competency Goals:

■ To advance physical and cognitive competence
■ To support social and emotional development and provide positive guidance

■ Functional Areas:

■ Physical
■ Cognitive
■ Social

Part I: Read from *Working with Young Children*

■ Chapter 4

Part II: Review What You Have Read

Directions: Answer the following questions.

1. Define the word *development*. _____

_____

_____

_____

2. What type of development is related to changes in bone thickness, vision, and hearing? _____

_____

3. List and explain three characteristics of development. _____

_____

_____

_____

_____

_____

_____

(Continued)

Copyright Goodheart-Willcox Co., Inc.

4. Explain why children's development depends on maturation. _____

_____

_____

_____

5. How should child care professionals react if they observe children with skill levels below norms on developmental scales? _____

_____

_____

_____

6. Why is it important for doctors and others who work with children to understand and check infants' reflexes?_____

_____

_____

_____

7. Why are infants able to crawl before they can creep? _____

_____

_____

_____

8. How do heredity and environment interact to influence cognitive development?_____

_____

_____

_____

9. Describe how to test children for an understanding of object permanence._____

_____

_____

_____

10. A toddler sees his or her mother mowing the lawn one day, then pretends to mow the lawn at the child care center. What is this called? _____

11. List and describe three factors that affect children's temperaments. _____

_____

_____

_____

12. List two examples of attachment behaviors._____

_____

_____

Copyright Goodheart-Willcox Co., Inc.

Part III: Observe What You Have Learned

Comparing Developmental Characteristics

■ Objectives

After completing this activity, you will be able to

- list developmental characteristics of an infant and a toddler
- describe methods caregivers use to support the development of infants and toddlers
- list equipment that promotes development
- compare the developmental skills of an infant and a toddler

■ Preparation

1. Arrange to observe an infant and a toddler. Use more than one visit to complete the activity, if necessary.

2. Study age-appropriate developmental traits described in the text.

■ Setting

Place where observation occurred _____

_____

Phone number _____

Time_____ to _____

Name of caregiver_____

Title _____

Date _____

Number of children present _____

Ages of children _____ `

■ The Observation

Observe an infant and a toddler. Record the developmental characteristics of each child. Refer to the developmental traits listed in the text.

(Continued)

Infant	Toddler
Physical characteristics _____ _____ _____ _____	Physical characteristics _____ _____ _____ _____
Cognitive characteristics _____ _____ _____ _____	Cognitive characteristics _____ _____ _____ _____
Social characteristics _____ _____ _____ _____	Social characteristics _____ _____ _____ _____
Emotional characteristics _____ _____ _____ _____	Emotional characteristics _____ _____ _____ _____

■ Review What You Have Observed

1. In your observations, what did caregivers do to encourage physical development? _____

   _____

   _____

   _____

   _____

   _____

2. In your observations, what did caregivers do to encourage cognitive development? _____

   _____

   _____

   _____

   _____

   _____

   _____

(Continued)

Copyright Goodheart-Willcox Co., Inc.

Review What You Have Observed (Cont.)

3. In your observations, what did caregivers do to encourage social-emotional development? _____

_____

_____

_____

_____

_____

_____

_____

4. List equipment you observed. Consider reasons caregivers chose individual pieces as well as the developmental skills they promote. _____

_____

_____

_____

_____

_____

_____

_____

_____

5. How did caregivers adjust play activities to children's skill levels? _____

_____

_____

_____

_____

_____

_____

_____

_____

Part IV: Apply What You Have Learned

1. Describe an observation of an infant's Moro reflex. _____

_____

_____

_____

(Continued)

Copyright Goodheart-Willcox Co., Inc.

Apply What You Have Learned (Cont.)

2. Describe an observation of an infant's grasping reflex. _____
_____
_____
_____
_____

3. Describe an observation of an infant who has learned object permanence. _____
_____
_____
_____
_____

4. Describe an observation of a toddler using deferred imitation. _____
_____
_____
_____
_____

5. Contrast the temperaments of two children you have observed. _____
_____
_____
_____
_____
_____
_____

6. Describe an observation of separation anxiety. _____
_____
_____

Copyright Goodheart-Willcox Co., Inc.

Understanding Two- and Three-Year-Olds

■ Competency Goals:

■ To advance physical and cognitive competence
■ To support social and emotional development and provide positive guidance

■ Functional Areas:

■ Physical
■ Cognitive
■ Social

Part I: Read from *Working with Young Children*

■ Chapter 5

Part II: Review What You Have Read

Directions: Answer the following questions.

1. What self-help skills can two-year-olds perform? _____

_____

_____

_____

_____

2. How does language comprehension differ from expressive language? _____

_____

_____

_____

_____

3. List behaviors typical of two-year-olds. _____

_____

_____

_____

_____

4. Describe the gross motor abilities of three-year-olds. _____

_____

_____

_____

_____

(Continued)

Copyright Goodheart-Willcox Co., Inc.

5. How is the thinking process of three-year-olds flawed? _____
   _____
   _____
   _____

6. Describe three characteristics of three-year-olds' expressive language. _____
   _____
   _____
   _____

7. How do the play activities of three-year-olds differ from those of two-year-olds? _____
   _____
   _____
   _____
   _____

8. How are three-year-olds aware of gender roles? _____
   _____
   _____
   _____

9. Why are three-year-olds less likely to become angry than two-year-olds? _____
   _____
   _____
   _____
   _____

10. Explain why three-year-olds commonly use statements like, "I can do it," or "Let me do it." ____
    _____
    _____
    _____
    _____
    _____

Copyright Goodheart-Willcox Co., Inc.

Part III: Observe What You Have Learned

■ Developmental Characteristics of Two- and Three-Year-Olds

■ Objectives

After completing this activity, you will be able to

- identify physical, cognitive, social, and emotional developmental characteristics of two- and three-year-olds
- identify equipment and activities used to promote development
- compare developmental characteristics of two- and three-year-olds

■ Preparation

1. Arrange to observe a two-year-old child. Use more than one visit to complete the activity, if necessary.

2. Review the developmental traits listed in the text.

■ Setting

Place where observation occurred _____

_____

Phone number _____

Time _____

Title _____

Date _____ to _____

Age of child _____

■ The Observation

Observe a two-year-old child. Record his or her developmental skills.

Motor skills _____

_____

_____

_____

_____

_____

_____

_____

_____

(Continued)

Copyright Goodheart-Willcox Co., Inc.

Observe What You Have Learned (Cont.)

Cognitive skills _____

_____

_____

_____

_____

_____

_____

_____

Social skills _____

_____

_____

_____

_____

_____

_____

_____

Emotional skills _____

_____

_____

_____

_____

_____

_____

_____

■ Review What You Have Observed

1. Describe the vocabulary of the two-year-old you observed. _____

_____

_____

_____

_____

_____

(Continued)

Copyright Goodheart-Willcox Co., Inc.

Review What You Have Observed (Cont.)

2. Compare the developmental abilities of the two-year-old you observed to developmental norms listed in the text. Describe how the child compares to norms for the age group. _____

_____

_____

_____

_____

_____

_____

3. List equipment the caregiver used (or had available to use) to promote development of the skills listed below.

Gross motor _____

_____

_____

Fine motor _____

_____

_____

Self-help _____

_____

_____

Expressive language _____

_____

_____

Language comprehension _____

_____

_____

Math readiness_____

_____

Social_____

_____

_____

Emotional _____

_____

_____

Copyright Goodheart-Willcox Co., Inc.

Part IV: Apply What You Have Learned

1. List developmentally appropriate activities for two-year-olds, then modify the activities for three-year-olds.

Two-Year-Olds	Three-Year-Olds
Physical development _____ _____ _____ _____	Physical development _____ _____ _____ _____
Cognitive development _____ _____ _____ _____	Cognitive development _____ _____ _____ _____
Social development _____ _____ _____ _____	Social development _____ _____ _____ _____
Emotional development _____ _____ _____ _____	Emotional development _____ _____ _____ _____

2. Compare the language skills of a two-year-old and a three-year-old. _____
_____
_____
_____

3. Compare the fine motor skills of a two-year-old and a three-year-old. _____
_____
_____
_____

4. Compare the self-help skills of a two-year-old and a three-year-old. _____
_____
_____

5. Describe a three-year-old's play activities. _____
_____
_____
_____

Copyright Goodheart-Willcox Co., Inc.

Understanding Four- and Five-Year-Olds

■ Competency Goals:

■ To advance physical and intellectual competence
■ To support social and emotional development and provide positive guidance

■ Functional Areas:

■ Physical
■ Cognitive
■ Social

Part I: Read from *Working with Young Children*

■ Chapter 6

Part II: Review What You Have Read

Directions: Answer the following questions.

1. Why are some physical skills now easier for four- and five-year-olds? _____

_____

_____

_____

_____

2. Why is understanding symbols important for developing more advanced cognitive skills? _____

_____

_____

_____

_____

3. Define *passive voice* and give an example of a passive voice sentence. _____

_____

_____

_____

_____

4. What must children understand before they can read?_____

_____

_____

_____

_____

(Continued)

Copyright Goodheart-Willcox Co., Inc.

5. What phonetic sounds do many preschoolers have trouble articulating?_____

_____

_____

_____

_____

6. Why do some preschool children stutter?_____

_____

_____

_____

_____

7. How does true counting differ from rote counting? _____

_____

_____

_____

_____

_____

8. Describe how preschoolers feel about friendships._____

_____

_____

_____

_____

9. Why might four- and five-year-olds appear especially fearful?_____

_____

_____

_____

10. How might caregivers help jealous children?_____

_____

_____

_____

Copyright Goodheart-Willcox Co., Inc.

Part III: Observe What You Have Learned

Developmental Characteristics of Four- and Five-Year-Olds

■ Objectives

After completing this activity, you will be able to

■ identify physical, cognitive, social, and emotional developmental characteristics of four- and five-year-olds
■ identify equipment and activities used to promote development
■ compare developmental characteristics of four- and five-year-olds

■ Preparation

1. Arrange to observe a four-year-old child. Use more than one visit to complete the activity, if necessary.

2. Review the developmental traits listed in the text.

■ Setting

Place where observation occurred _____

_____

Phone number _____

Time _____ to _____

Name of caregiver_____

Title _____

Date _____

Age of child _____

■ The Observation

Observe a four-year-old child. Record his or her developmental skills.

Motor skills_____

_____

_____

_____

_____

_____

Cognitive skills _____

_____

_____

_____

_____

_____

(Continued)

Copyright Goodheart-Willcox Co., Inc.

Observe What You Have Learned (Cont.)

Social skills _____

_____

_____

_____

Emotional skills _____

_____

_____

_____

_____

■ Review What You Have Observed

1. Describe the four-year-old's physical appearance. Compare it to a five-year-old's appearance. _____

_____

_____

_____

_____

2. Describe the four-year-old's writing skills. _____

_____

_____

_____

_____

3. Give examples of the four-year-old's use of grammar. What difficulties did he or she have?_____

_____

_____

_____

_____

4. Did the child become frightened, angry, jealous, or sad during the observation? Describe what evoked the feelings and how the child expressed them. _____

_____

_____

_____

_____

(Continued)

Copyright Goodheart-Willcox Co., Inc.

5. In your observation, was the child cooperative and helpful? List examples of his or her eagerness to please.

_____

_____

_____

_____

_____

6. List equipment the caregiver used to promote development of the areas listed below.

Physical development _____

_____

_____

_____

_____

Cognitive development _____

_____

_____

_____

_____

Social development _____

_____

_____

_____

_____

Emotional development_____

_____

_____

_____

_____

Part IV: Apply What You Have Learned

1. Compare the language skills of a four-year-old and a five-year-old. _____

_____

_____

_____

_____

(Continued)

Apply What You Have Learned (Cont.)

2. Compare fine motor skills of a four-year-old and a five-year-old. _____

_____

_____

_____

_____

_____

3. Compare self-help skills of a four-year-old and a five-year-old. _____

_____

_____

_____

_____

_____

4. Describe a five-year-old's play activities. _____

_____

_____

_____

_____

5. List developmentally appropriate activities for four-year-olds, then modify the activities for five-year-olds.

_____

_____

_____

_____

_____

6. Using your text as a reference, record skills and equipment/materials to promote the development of four- and five-year-olds.

Four-Year-Olds

Gross Motor Skills	
Skill catches beanbag with hands	Equipment/Materials beanbag

Fine Motor Skills	
Skill builds a three-block bridge from model	Equipment/Materials floor and table building blocks

(Continued)

Copyright Goodheart-Willcox Co., Inc.

Apply What You Have Learned (Cont.)

Four-Year-Olds

Self-Help Skills	
Skill buckles belt	Equipment/Materials belts in dramatic play area

Expressive Language Skills	
Skill	Equipment/Materials

Language Comprehension Skills	
Skill	Equipment/Materials

Math Readiness Skills	
Skill	Equipment/Materials

Social-Emotional Skills	
Skill	Equipment/Materials

(Continued)

Copyright Goodheart-Willcox Co., Inc.

Five-Year-Olds

Gross Motor Skills	
Skill _____	Equipment/Materials _____
_____	_____
_____	_____
_____	_____

Fine Motor Skills	
Skill _____	Equipment/Materials _____
_____	_____
_____	_____
_____	_____

Self-Help Skills	
Skill _____	Equipment/Materials _____
_____	_____
_____	_____
_____	_____

Expressive Language Skills	
Skill _____	Equipment/Materials _____
_____	_____
_____	_____
_____	_____

Language Comprehension Skills	
Skill _____	Equipment/Materials _____
_____	_____
_____	_____
_____	_____

Math Readiness Skills	
Skill _____	Equipment/Materials _____
_____	_____
_____	_____
_____	_____

Social-Emotional Skills	
Skill _____	Equipment/Materials _____
_____	_____
_____	_____
_____	_____

Copyright Goodheart-Willcox Co., Inc.

Middle Childhood

■ Competency Goals:

■ To advance physical and intellectual competence
■ To support social and emotional development and provide positive guidance

■ Functional Areas:

■ Physical
■ Cognitive
■ Social
■ Guidance

Part I: Read from *Working with Young Children*

■ Chapter 7

Part II: Review What You Have Read

Directions: Answer the following questions.

1. Define the term *middle childhood.* _____

_____

_____

2. Describe physical development during middle childhood. _____

_____

_____

_____

_____

_____

_____

_____

3. Describe the changes in a child's weight between ages 6 and 12. _____

_____

_____

_____

_____

_____

_____

(Continued)

Copyright Goodheart-Willcox Co., Inc.

Review What You Have Read (Cont.)

4. What does improved finger dexterity enable school-age children to do?

_____

_____

_____

_____

_____

_____

5. Why is middle childhood often one of the healthiest periods for children?_____

_____

_____

_____

6. What is the difference between the terms *farsighted* and *nearsighted*? _____

_____

_____

_____

_____

_____

7. How can teachers promote good dental health? _____

_____

_____

_____

_____

_____

8. List the factors that contribute to obesity._____

_____

_____

_____

_____

_____

(Continued)

Copyright Goodheart-Willcox Co., Inc.

Review What You Have Read (Cont.)

9. Describe and provide examples of seriation and classification. _____
_____
_____
_____
_____
_____
_____

10. Compare friendships during the preschool years to those during middle childhood. _____
_____
_____
_____
_____
_____

11. What gender differences exist in activity preferences during middle childhood? _____
_____
_____
_____
_____
_____
_____
_____

12. List how children benefit from participation in competitive sports. _____
_____
_____
_____
_____
_____

Copyright Goodheart-Willcox Co., Inc.

Part III: Observe What You Have Learned

Observation A: Observing Developmental Characteristics of Six- and Seven-Year-Olds

■ Objectives

After completing this activity, you will be able to

- ■ observe the physical appearance of a six- or seven-year-old child
- ■ observe the development of a six- or seven-year-old
- ■ describe the types of activities for which the child needed an adult's assistance

■ Preparation

1. Make arrangements to observe a six- or seven-year-old child in an elementary school or during after-school child care.

2. Review the developmental characteristics of this age child in the textbook.

■ Setting

Place where observation occurred _____

_____

Address _____

Phone number _____

Contact person _____

Date _____

Time_____ to _____

Name of child _____

Birthdate _____

Age _____Height_____Weight _____

Other information _____

_____

■ The Observation

Respond to the items listed below during your observation of the children.

1. Describe the child's physical appearance._____

   _____

   _____

   _____

   _____

2. How does the child 's weight and height compare with other children the same age? _____

   _____

   _____

   _____

   _____

(Continued)

Copyright Goodheart-Willcox Co., Inc.

Observe What You Have Learned (Cont.)

3. Describe the child's fine motor and gross motor skills. _____

_____

_____

_____

4. Compare the child's motor skills with those expected at this age.

_____

_____

_____

5. What evidence have you observed of the child's thinking processes? _____

_____

_____

_____

_____

6. Describe the child's language skills. _____

_____

_____

_____

_____

7. Describe the child's social and emotional development. _____

_____

_____

_____

_____

8. How does the child compare with other children in the same age group?_____

_____

_____

_____

_____

9. Describe the child's behavior. Note whether it appears typical or atypical of children this age._____

_____

_____

_____

_____

Copyright Goodheart-Willcox Co., Inc.

Observation B: Observing Developmental Characteristics of Eight- and Nine-Year-Olds

■ Objectives

After completing this activity, you will be able to

- observe general characteristics of eight-year-old and/or nine-year-old children
- recall the children's physical, social, emotional and cognitive development
- describe the types of activities the children seem to enjoy
- describe the relationship of the children with one another and adults
- describe any gender differences noted between the boys and the girls

■ Preparation

1. Make arrangements to observe a group of eight- and nine-year-old children in a local elementary school or during after-school child care.

2. Review the development of this age child in the textbook.

■ Setting

Place where observation occurred

_____

Address _____

Phone number _____

Contact person _____

Date _____

Time_____ to _____

Number of children _____Number of adults _____

Other information _____

_____

■ The Observation

Observe the group of children for at least one hour. Then respond to the following statements.

1. Describe incidents or examples of general characteristics of eight- and nine-year-olds listed in the text that you observed._____

_____

_____

_____

_____

_____

_____

_____

_____

_____

(Continued)

Copyright Goodheart-Willcox Co., Inc.

Observe What You Have Learned (Cont.)

2. List the physical skills and motor behaviors that the children demonstrated. _____

_____

_____

_____

_____

_____

_____

_____

3. Describe the relationship of the children with one another and the adult._____

_____

_____

_____

_____

_____

_____

4. Describe the types of activities the children seemed to enjoy._____

_____

_____

_____

_____

_____

5. Describe any gender differences in activity preferences and social relationships between the girls and boys that you observed. _____

_____

_____

_____

_____

_____

_____

Copyright Goodheart-Willcox Co., Inc.

Observation C: Observing Developmental Characteristics of Ten- and Eleven-Year-Olds

■ Objectives

After completing this activity, you will be able to

- observe general characteristics of ten-year-old and/or eleven-year-old children
- recall the children's physical, social, emotional, and cognitive development
- describe the types of activities the children seem to enjoy
- describe the relationship of the children with one another and adults
- describe any noted gender differences between the boys and the girls

■ Preparation

1. Make arrangements to observe a group of ten- and eleven-year-old children in a local primary school.

2. Review the development of this age child in the textbook.

■ Setting

Place where observation occurred _____

_____

Address _____

Phone number _____

Contact person _____

Date _____

Time_____ to _____

Number of children_____Number of adults _____

Other information _____

_____

■ The Observation

Observe the group of children for at least one hour. Then respond to the following statements.

1. Describe incidents or examples of general characteristics of ten- and eleven-year-olds listed in the text that you observed._____

_____

_____

_____

_____

_____

_____

_____

_____

_____

(Continued)

Copyright Goodheart-Willcox Co., Inc.

2. List below the physical skills and motor behaviors that the children demonstrated. _____

_____

_____

_____

_____

_____

_____

_____

_____

_____

_____

3. Describe the relationship of the children with one another and the adult. _____

_____

_____

_____

_____

_____

_____

_____

_____

_____

4. Describe the types of activities the children seemed to enjoy. _____

_____

_____

_____

_____

_____

_____

_____

_____

(Continued)

Copyright Goodheart-Willcox Co., Inc.

5. Describe the gender differences in activity preferences and social relationships between the girls and boys that you observed. _____

_____

_____

_____

_____

_____

_____

Part IV: Apply What You Have Learned

1. Compare the development of six-, seven-, eight-, nine-, ten-, and eleven-year-olds. _____

_____

_____

_____

_____

_____

_____

2. Describe an observation of a child who has learned conservation. _____

_____

_____

_____

_____

_____

_____

3. List the benefits for children participating in team sports. _____

_____

_____

_____

_____

_____

_____

(Continued)

Copyright Goodheart-Willcox Co., Inc.

Apply What You Have Learned (Cont.)

4. Describe how children learn moral development. _____

_____

_____

_____

_____

_____

_____

5. Describe how games are important for the children's development. _____

_____

_____

_____

_____

_____

_____

6. Describe why friendships are important during the school-age years. _____

_____

_____

_____

_____

_____

_____

7. Describe an observation of a child during middle childhood engaging in social comparison. _____

_____

_____

_____

_____

_____

_____

_____

_____

(Continued)

Copyright Goodheart-Willcox Co., Inc.

8. Describe the effect of obesity on children during middle childhood. _____

_____

_____

_____

_____

_____

_____

_____

9. Describe an observation of the gender differences in physical development during middle childhood. _____

_____

_____

_____

_____

_____

Copyright Goodheart-Willcox Co., Inc.

Preparing the Environment

■ **Competency Goal:**

■ To establish and maintain a safe, healthy learning environment

■ **Functional Areas:**

■ Learning Environment
■ Guidance

Part I: Read from *Working with Young Children*

■ Chapter 8

Part II: Review What You Have Read

Directions: Answer the following questions.

1. List the six goals for a well-planned space. _____

_____

_____

_____

_____

_____

_____

2. How can small children comfortably use adult-sized toilets and sinks? _____

_____

_____

_____

_____

3. List one advantage and one disadvantage of hanging blinds or drapes in a classroom. _____

_____

_____

_____

_____

_____

(Continued)

Review What You Have Read (Cont.)

4. What is acoustic material? Give an example. _____

_____

_____

_____

5. Why should lockers or cubbies be placed near the center's entrance? _____

_____

_____

_____

_____

_____

6. Compare how cool colors and warm colors affect the appearance of a room._____

_____

_____

_____

7. Why is group size an important factor to consider when arranging space?_____

_____

_____

_____

8. What should caregivers consider when planning activity areas? _____

_____

_____

9. What guidelines should caregivers follow to best use play yard space? _____

_____

_____

_____

_____

_____

10. List advantages and disadvantages of having a chain-link fence. _____

_____

_____

_____

_____

Copyright Goodheart-Willcox Co., Inc.

Part III: Observe What You Have Learned

Observation A: Center Physical Space

■ Objectives

After completing this activity, you will be able to
■ draw and describe the physical space of a child care center
■ explain the locations of the general center areas

■ Preparation

1. Arrange to visit a child care, preschool, Head Start, or kindergarten early childhood program.

2. You will need a pencil and ruler to draw the floor plan.

■ Setting

Place where observation occurred _____

_____

■ The Observation

On the graph paper provided, draw a floor plan of the facilities. Include the following general areas:

1. entrance

2. director's office

3. isolation area

4. kitchen or kitchenette

5. staff room (if available)

6. classrooms

7. bathrooms

Copyright Goodheart-Willcox Co., Inc.

Center Floor Plan

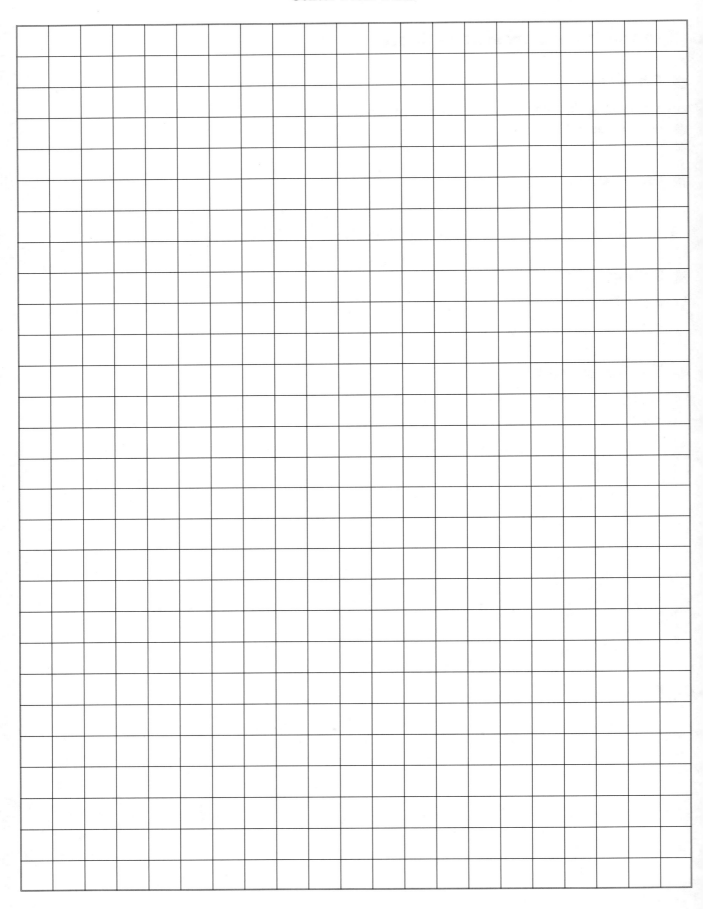

Copyright Goodheart-Willcox Co., Inc.

■ Review What You Have Observed

1. Describe the entrance. Was it appealing and attractive? If not, how could it be improved? _____

_____

_____

_____

2. Describe the director's office. Was it conveniently located? If not, what location would be more convenient?

_____

_____

_____

3. Describe the location and appearance of the isolation area. Could this area be improved? Explain. _____

_____

_____

_____

4. Describe the location of the kitchen. Was it conveniently located? If not, what location would be more convenient? _____

_____

_____

_____

5. Describe the location of the bathroom. Was it conveniently located adjacent to the classroom? _____

_____

_____

_____

6. Describe the place available for a sick child to rest. Is it quiet and isolated? Are adults able to be near the child? Explain._____

_____

_____

_____

Observation B: Play Yard Space

■ Objectives

After completing this activity, you will be able to

■ draw an outdoor play area

■ explain the positioning of the play equipment and space in the area observed

■ Preparation

1. Arrange to visit an early childhood center with an outdoor play area.

2. You will need a pencil and ruler to draw the outdoor play area.

■ Setting

Place where observation occurred _____

_____

The Observation

On the graph that follows, draw the shape of the outdoor activity area. Then draw all the outdoor equipment and surface paths.

Copyright Goodheart-Willcox Co., Inc.

Play Yard Arrangement

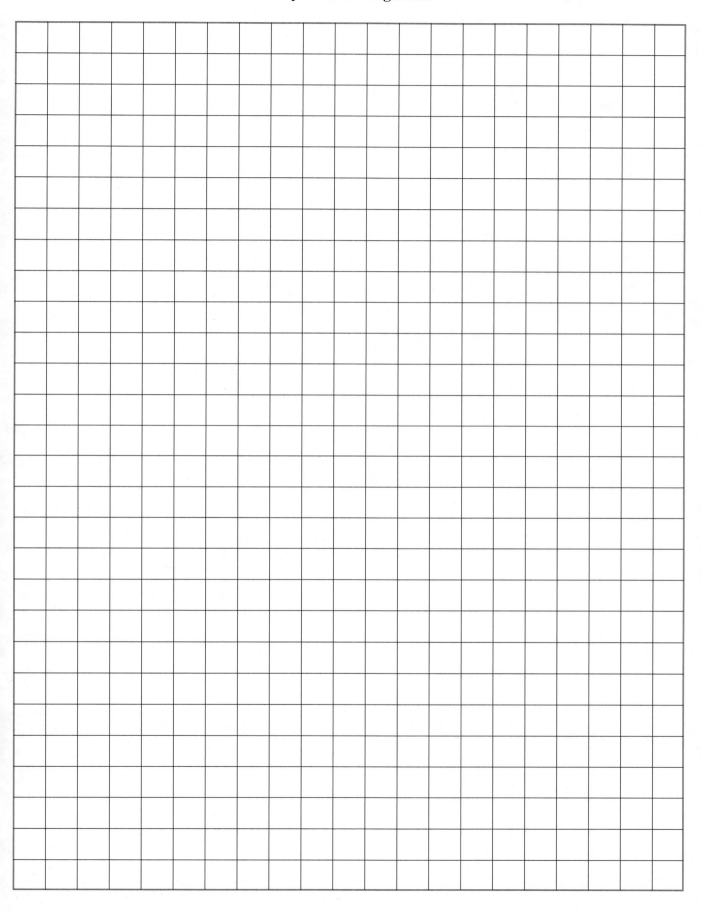

Copyright Goodheart-Willcox Co., Inc.

■ Review What You Have Observed

1. Describe the play yard surface. Was it appropriate or inappropriate for use with young children? Explain.___

   _____

   _____

   _____

   _____

2. Describe the fencing used. Explain why it was or was not aesthetically pleasing. _____

   _____

   _____

   _____

   _____

3. Did landscaping make the play yard aesthetically pleasing? If used, describe. _____

   _____

   _____

   _____

   _____

4. Were surface paths included on which children might drive or ride wheeled toys? If so, describe their locations.

   _____

   _____

   _____

   _____

5. Was the stationary equipment placed in the best location? Explain. _____

   _____

   _____

   _____

   _____

Copyright Goodheart-Willcox Co., Inc.

Part IV: Apply What You Have Learned

1. Review the traffic patterns of your classroom or a classroom you have observed. Are they appropriate?____

_____

_____

_____

_____

_____

_____

_____

2. What is the predominant color of your classroom or a classroom you have observed? How does it affect the appearance of the room? _____

_____

_____

_____

_____

_____

_____

_____

_____

3. If you could change the color of the room described above, what color would you select? Why?_____

_____

_____

_____

_____

_____

_____

_____

_____

_____

(Continued)

Copyright Goodheart-Willcox Co., Inc.

4. Describe the location of the basic activity areas of your classroom or a classroom you have observed. Are they logically arranged according to function? Are wet and dry areas separated? Are active and quiet areas separated? Evaluate the location of the areas, and suggest any improvements you would make. _____

_____

_____

_____

_____

_____

_____

_____

_____

_____

_____

_____

_____

_____

_____

_____

_____

5. Describe the outdoor play area of a center you have observed. Is the play yard space used efficiently? Why or why not? _____

_____

_____

_____

_____

_____

_____

_____

6. Are indoor and outdoor spaces arranged to limit disruptive behavior? Explain. _____

_____

_____

_____

_____

Copyright Goodheart-Willcox Co., Inc.

Selecting Toys, Equipment, and Educational Materials

■ **Competency Goal:**

■ To establish and maintain a safe, healthy learning environment

■ **Functional Area:**

■ Learning Environment

Part I: Read from *Working with Young Children*

■ Chapter 9

Part II: Review What You Have Read

Directions: Answer the following questions.

1. Why is supervision a criteria for selecting toys? _____

_____

_____

_____

2. Why should caregivers avoid purchasing spectator toys? _____

_____

_____

_____

3. Define the term *developmental age*. _____

_____

_____

_____

_____

4. Why must caregivers provide nonsexist and multicultural toys? _____

_____

_____

5. List four questions caregivers should ask regarding the safety of a toy. _____

_____

_____

_____

_____

(Continued)

Copyright Goodheart-Willcox Co., Inc.

6. Why are balloons dangerous toys for young children? _____

_____

_____

7. How can play yard equipment be arranged on the play yard to meet the needs of mixed age groups?

_____

_____

8. List six basic play yard equipment dangers. _____

_____

_____

_____

_____

_____

_____

_____

_____

_____

9. To report an unsafe toy or piece of equipment, which government agency should be contacted? _____

_____

10. Define a co-op. Why are co-ops usually formed? _____

_____

_____

_____

11. List two examples of consumable supplies. _____

_____

_____

(Continued)

Copyright Goodheart-Willcox Co., Inc.

Part III: Observe What You Have Learned

Observation A: Evaluating a Toy

Objectives

After completing this activity, you will be able to
- observe a child interacting with a toy
- evaluate a toy

■ Preparation

1. Select a toy to evaluate.

2. Review the toy evaluation criteria listed below.

■ Setting

Place where observation occurred _____

_____

Name of caregiver_____

Title _____

Date _____

Age of child _____

Equipment Being Evaluated _____

Time _____ to _____

■ The Observation

Observe a child interacting with a toy you choose to evaluate. Use the criteria listed below to evaluate the toy.

	Yes	No
1. Does the toy support program goals?		
2. Does the toy add balance to existing materials and equipment?		
3. Can the toy be used in available classroom space?		
4. Does the toy require a great deal of supervision?		
5. Is the toy easy to maintain?		
6. Is the toy durable?		
7. Can the toy be purchased in sufficient quantities?		
8. Does the toy require the involvement of the child?		
9. Is the toy apprpriate for the developmental stages of the children who will be using it?		
10. Will the toy be of interest to the children?		
11. Is the toy nonviolent?		
12. Is the toy nonsexist?		
13. Is the toy multicultural?		
14. Is the toy safe?		

■ Review What You Have Observed

1. From your observations, did the toy maintain the child's interest? Describe why or why not. _____

_____

_____

_____

_____

2. Would you purchase this toy for your classroom? Justify your answer. _____

_____

_____

_____

_____

Observation B: Evaluating a Swing Set

■ Objectives

After completing this activity, you will be able to
- identify swing set safety features
- evaluate a children's swing set

■ Preparation

1. Arrange to visit a children's play area that contains a swing set.

2. Review the criteria listed on the chart that follows.

■ Setting

Place where observation occurred _____

_____

Date _____

Copyright Goodheart-Willcox Co., Inc.

■ The Observation

Use the criteria listed below to evaluate a swing set.

	Yes	No
1. Is the construction durable?		
2. Is it an appropriate height?		
3. Does it complement existing equipment in function?		
4. Are the exercise rings less than 5 inches or more than 10 inches in diameter?		
5. Is it free of open S-rings?		
6. Are seats on swings made of plastic or canvas?		
7. Is it free of exposed nuts and bolts?		
8. Is it free of sharp edges?		
9. Can the equipment be properly anchored?		
10. Is the equipment easy to maintain?		
11. Is the frame stable?		

■ Review What You Have Observed

1. After completing the checklist, do you conclude the swing set is safe or unsafe? Justify your answer._____

_____

_____

_____

_____

_____

2. Could the manufacturer improve this piece of equipment? Explain your answer._____

_____

_____

_____

_____

3. Would you purchase this swing set? Explain._____

_____

_____

_____

_____

Part IV: Apply What You Have Learned

1. Describe potential play yard equipment dangers you have observed. _____

_____

_____

_____

_____

_____

2. Describe potentially dangerous toys you have observed in a classroom. _____

_____

_____

_____

_____

_____

_____

3. Describe several sexist toys and explain how you would replace them with nonsexist toys. Why is this important? _____

_____

_____

_____

_____

_____

_____

4. Describe several multicultural toys you feel should be provided in a child care center. Explain why you would provide these. _____

_____

_____

_____

_____

_____

_____

_____

_____

_____

Copyright Goodheart-Willcox Co., Inc.

Promoting Children's Safety

■ **Competency Goal:**

■ To establish and maintain a safe, healthy learning environment

■ **Functional Areas:**

■ Safe
■ Healthy
■ Learning Environment

Part I: Read from *Working with Young Children*

■ Chapter 10

Part II: Review What You Have Read

Directions: Answer the following questions.

1. List at least three basic objectives for providing a safe environment for children. _____

_____

_____

_____

_____

_____

_____

2. Why is constant supervision in a preschool classroom necessary? _____

_____

_____

_____

_____

3. Provide at least two examples of safety limits._____

_____

_____

_____

_____

4. List one way centers should keep their vehicles safe for children and adults. _____

_____

_____

(Continued)

Copyright Goodheart-Willcox Co., Inc.

5. What signs indicate a fire extinguisher needs to be replaced immediately? _____

_____

_____

_____

6. What substance can you give a child to induce vomiting? _____

7. Define the phrase *nonaccidental physical injury*. _____

_____

_____

8. List signs that may indicate child neglect. _____

_____

_____

9. List two behavioral patterns exhibited by emotionally abused children. _____

_____

_____

_____

_____

10. How can caregivers teach children to resist sexual attacks? _____

_____

_____

_____

_____

_____

11. List four situations for which child care center staff can be held liable. _____

_____

_____

_____

_____

12. What is the privacy law? _____

_____

_____

Copyright Goodheart-Willcox Co., Inc.

Part III: Observe What You Have Learned

Observation A: Indoor Safety Checklist

■ Objectives

After completing this activity, you will be able to
■ check for important indoor safety precautions in a child care setting
■ identify items that are important for maintaining a safe indoor environment for children

■ Preparation

1. Arrange to visit a child care center or preschool.

2. Review the safety criteria outlined on the checklist below.

■ Setting

Place where observation occurred _____

_____

Name of caregiver_____

Title _____

■ The Observation

Using the criteria listed, observe to see if the center meets adequate safety conditions, then check the appropriate column.

	Yes	No
1. Exit passageways and exits are free from furniture and equipment.		
2. Locks on bathroom doors and toilet stalls can be opened from the outside and are readily accessible to center staff.		
3. Protective covers are on all electrical outlets.		
4. Permanent wiring is used rather than lengthy extension cords.		
5. Each wall outlet contains no more than two electrical appliances.		
6. Monthly staff inspections are conducted on facilities.		
7. A fire evacuation plan is posted.		
8. Fire drills are conducted at least monthly, some of which are unannounced.		
9. Flammable, combustible, and dangerous materials are marked and stored in areas accessible only to staff.		
10. First aid supplies are evident.		
11. Children are restricted to floors with grade-level exits (no stairs).		
12. The basement door is kept closed.		
13. There is no storage under stairs.		

(Continued)

	Yes	No
14. Fire extinguishers are in place and checked regularly.		
15. Smoke alarms and fire extinguishers are checked at least monthly.		
16. Fire alarm system meets local regulations.		
17. Premises are clean, indicating housekeeping is maintained.		
18. Dangerous pieces of equipment (knives, scissors, etc.) are kept out of children's reach.		
19. The hot water heater is set low enough so children are not burned while washing their hands.		
20. Medicine, poisonous substances, and the first aid kit are kept out of children's reach.		
21. Floors are kept clean of spills and litter.		
22. Stairway handrails are at children's height.		
23. Lighting on stairways is adequate.		
24. Stairs are covered with a nonslip surface.		
25. Emergency information for staff and children is near phone.		
26. Storage units are stable and will not slide or fall.		
27. Strict sanitary procedures are followed during food preparation.		

■ Review What You Have Observed

1. Did the center meet all the safety criteria? If not, describe what center personnel must do to make the environment safer for children. _____

_____

_____

_____

Observation B: Outdoor Safety Checklist

■ Objectives

After completing this activity, you will be able to
■ check for important outdoor safety precautions in a child care setting
■ identify items that are important for maintaining a safe outdoor environment for children

■ Preparation

1. Arrange to visit a child care center with an outdoor play yard designed for preschool children.

2. Review the criteria outlined on the checklist that follows.

Copyright Goodheart-Willcox Co., Inc.

■ Setting

Place where observation occurred _____

_____

Name of caregiver_____

Title _____

■ The Observation

Using the criteria listed, observe to see if the play yard meets adequate safety conditions.

	Yes	No
1. Play yard is fenced in.		
2. If a gate is provided, the lock is in good condition.		
3. Surfaces are free from clutter.		
4. Equipment is age-appropriate.		
5. Construction of equipment is durable.		
6. Nuts and bolts are covered to prevent injury.		
7. Sharp edges on equipment are filed.		
8. Equipment is properly anchored.		
9. S-rings are closed.		
10. Cushioned surfaces are under play structures.		
11. Shade is available.		
12. Plants, shrubs, and trees are free from thorns or sharp edges.		
13. Plants, shrubs, and flowers are nonpoisonous.		
14. Sand area is covered when not in use.		
15. Sand is free from insects and animal litter.		
16. Water is drained from outdoor table when not in use.		

■ Review What You Have Observed

1. Did the play yard meet all safety criteria? If not, describe what personnel must do to make the environment safer for children. _____

_____

_____

_____

Copyright Goodheart-Willcox Co., Inc.

Part IV: Apply What You Have Learned

1. What safety limits would you have in your classroom? _____

   _____

   _____

   _____

   _____

   _____

2. Describe the evacuation procedure you would use in your classroom. _____

   _____

   _____

   _____

   _____

   _____

3. How would you address protection education in your classroom? _____

   _____

   _____

   _____

   _____

   _____

4. Where is the fire extinguisher located in a classroom you have observed? Is it adequate for all types of fires? Why or why not? _____

   _____

   _____

   _____

   _____

   _____

5. Review the outdoor play yard where you observed. List improvements that would protect children's safety.

   _____

   _____

   _____

   _____

   _____

Copyright Goodheart-Willcox Co., Inc.

Planning Nutritious Meals and Snacks

Competency Goal:

◼ To establish and maintain a safe, healthy learning environment

Functional Areas:

◼ Safe
◼ Healthy
◼ Learning Environment

Part I: Read from *Working with Young Children*

◼ Chapter 11

Part II: Review What You Have Read

Directions: Answer the following questions.

1. List at least three program goals concerning nutrition. _____

_____

_____

_____

2. Describe how proper nutrition builds and maintains a strong body. _____

_____

_____

_____

_____

3. Compare undernutrition and malnutrition. _____

_____

_____

_____

_____

4. What effect can obesity have upon children? _____

_____

_____

_____

(Continued)

Copyright Goodheart-Willcox Co., Inc.

5. Foods from what five groups are needed to nourish the body? _____

_____

_____

_____

_____

6. How many servings of dairy products do young children need each day? _____

7. Why should caregivers serve fruits and vegetables raw or slightly cooked?_____

_____

_____

8. What factors affect how much children enjoy their meals? _____

_____

_____

9. Why might soup be difficult for young children to eat?_____

_____

_____

10. List factors that determine whether a center serves breakfast._____

_____

_____

Part III: Observe What You Have Learned

Serving Adequate Meals

Objectives

After completing this activity, you will be able to
- evaluate the serving sizes of items served for breakfast or lunch at a child care center
- evaluate the menu on the basis of the Food Guide Pyramid for Young Children.

Preparation

1. Arrange to visit a child care center or kindergarten program during breakfast or lunch.

2. Review the text, then complete the Recommended Serving Size for Age column on the chart that follows.

(Continued)

Copyright Goodheart-Willcox Co., Inc.

Observe What You Have Learned (Cont.)

Setting

Place where observation occurred _____

_____

Name of caregiver _____

Title _____

Number of children present _____

Ages of children _____

Meal being observed _____

Time _____ to _____

The Observation

Observe caregivers serving breakfast or lunch at a center. Record foods and serving sizes in the chart below.

Food	Serving Size	Recommended Serving Size for Age

Below, list the menu items served according to the food groups in the Food Guide Pyramid for Young Children.

Grain group _____

_____

Vegetable group _____

_____

Fruit group _____

_____

Meat group _____

_____

Milk group _____

_____

Fats and sweets group _____

_____

Review What You Have Observed

1. Were foods from all food groups adequately provided? If not, how could the menu be improved?_____

_____

_____

_____

_____

_____

2. Were serving sizes provided appropriate for the ages of the children? If not, what changes would you suggest?_____

_____

_____

_____

_____

_____

Copyright Goodheart-Willcox Co., Inc.

Part IV: Apply What You Have Learned

1. Using the Food Guide Pyramid for Young Children, plan three daily menus on the chart below. Make the meals nutritious for children in a child care setting. In the last row of boxes, list the number of servings each menu provides from the five food groups.

	Menu A	Menu B	Menu C
Breakfast			
Lunch			
Snack			
Servings menu provides	Grain group ____ servings (6 recommended daily) Vegetable group ____ servings (3 recommended daily) Fruit group ____ servings (2 recommended daily) Meat group ____ servings (2 recommended daily) Milk group ____ servings (2 recommended daily)	Grain group ____ servings (6 recommended daily) Vegetable group ____ servings (3 recommended daily) Fruit group ____ servings (2 recommended daily) Meat group ____ servings (2 recommended daily) Milk group ____ servings (2 recommended daily)	Grain group ____ servings (6 recommended daily) Vegetable group ____ servings (3 recommended daily) Fruit group ____ servings (2 recommended daily) Meat group ____ servings (2 recommended daily) Milk group ____ servings (2 recommended daily)

(Continued)

Copyright Goodheart-Willcox Co., Inc.

2. Describe the food preferences of a child you have observed. Why do you think the child liked these foods?

_____

_____

_____

_____

_____

_____

_____

_____

_____

_____

3. Is the eating atmosphere pleasant? How do caregivers make an effort to create a pleasant atmosphere? Do their efforts affect the children's eating habits? Explain. _____

_____

_____

_____

_____

_____

_____

_____

_____

_____

_____

_____

4. Are children always attended by an authorized adult during meals? Explain. _____

_____

_____

_____

_____

_____

_____

_____

_____

_____

_____

Copyright Goodheart-Willcox Co., Inc.

Guiding Children's Health

■ Competency Goal:

■ To establish and maintain a safe, healthy learning environment

■ Functional Area:

■ Healthy

Part I: Read from *Working with Young Children*

■ Chapter 12

Part II: Review What You Have Read

Directions: Answer the following questions.

1. What can caregivers learn from children's preadmission medical examinations? _____

   _____

   _____

   _____

2. What can cause foodborne illnesses? _____

3. How can caregivers prevent food contamination and foodborne illness? _____

   _____

   _____

   _____

   _____

4. Contrast a closed wound and an open wound. _____

   _____

   _____

   _____

5. Name the most common type of closed wound. _____

6. How do children usually get abrasions? _____

   _____

7. Describe open wounds that require medical attention. _____

   _____

   _____

   _____

   _____

(Continued)

8. List and describe the three classes of burns. _____

_____

_____

_____

_____

_____

9. What causes anaphylactic shock? Describe its symptoms. _____

_____

_____

_____

_____

10. What actions should a caregiver take if a child knocks out a permanent tooth? _____

_____

_____

_____

_____

11. How is head lice spread? _____

_____

Part III: Observe What You Have Learned

Observation A: Staff Health Practices

■ Objectives

After completing this activity, you will be able to
■ identify health practices that prevent food contamination and foodborne illness
■ describe practices that need to be followed to prevent bacteria growth and protect children's health

■ Preparation

1. Arrange to visit a child care center when the center staff is preparing a meal.

2. Read the checklist of health practices on the following page.

(Continued)

Copyright Goodheart-Willcox Co., Inc.

Observe What You Have Learned (Cont.)

■ Setting

Place where observation occurred _____

_____

Name of caregiver_____

Title _____

Ages of children _____ Meal being observed _____

■ The Observation

As you observe food preparation, check the appropriate column for each health practice. If you cannot observe the food preparation process, ask the cook or director whether each practice is followed.

Health Practices	Not Observed	Yes	No
1. Adults and children thoroughly wash hands with liquid soap after each visit to the bathroom.			
2. Hands are washed with liquid soap after coughing, sneezing, rubbing nose, or handling tissues.			
3. Disposable tissues are used.			
4. Tissues are discarded in a closed, plastic-lined container once used.			
5. Children and adults cover their mouths when coughing or sneezing.			
6. Only healthy staff prepare food.			
7. Only commercially prepared canned goods are used.			
8. Foods are quickly chilled and refrigerated.			
9. Hot foods held above 140°F.			
10. Hands are washed before preparing food and eating.			
11. Equipment and hands are thoroughly washed after working with raw meat and eggs.			
12. Cleaning pail is always washed.			
13. Flies, insects, and rodents are controlled.			
14. Foods are cooled in the refrigerator, not at room temperature.			
15. Cans with dents along side seams or with off-odors are discarded.			
16. Meats with off-odors or slimy surfaces are always thrown away.			
17. Foods are thawed only in the refrigerator.			
18. Perishable foods are prepared just prior to serving.			

Copyright Goodheart-Willcox Co., Inc.

■ Review What You Have Observed

1. Were you able to answer yes to all statements? If not, how might the center improve its health practices?

_____

_____

_____

Observation B: First Aid Kit

■ Objectives

After completing this activity, you will be able to
■ identify the items needed in a first aid kit
■ describe replacement items needed in a first aid kit

■ Preparation

1. Arrange to visit a child care center.

2. Read the first aid kit items listed on the chart that follows.

■ Setting

Place where observation occurred _____

_____

Name of caregiver_____

Title _____

■ The Observation

Check contents of the first aid kit. If any replacements are needed, tell the director or caregiver.

Quantity	Item	Complete	Replace
1	Quick reference first aid manual		
15 each	Individual adhesive bandages in one-half inch, three-quarter inch, and round spot sizes		
10	Two-by-two-inch sterile first aid dressings, individually packaged for burns and open wounds		
10	Four-by-four-inch sterile first aid dressings		
1 roll	Guaze bandage, two inches by five yards		
2 rolls	Adhesive tape or surgical tape, one-inch wide		
20	Disposable paper tissues		
1 bar	Mild soap for cleaning scratches and wounds		
1 pair	Tweezers for removing splinters		

Copyright Goodheart-Willcox Co., Inc.

Observe What You Have Learned (Cont.)

Quantity	Item	Complete	Replace
1 pair	Scissors for cutting tape and bandages		
1 package	Safety pins		
1 tube	Hydrocortisone cream for insect bites		
5	One-ounce bottles of syrup of ipecac		
1	Flashlight		
1	Synthetic ice pack		
1	Box of temperature strips for use on the child's forehead or digital thermometer		
20	Alcohol wipes		
20	Cotton swabs		
1 package	Absorbent cotton balls		
1 bottle	Antibacterial skin cleaner		

■ Review What You Have Observed

1. Did the first aid kit contain all the recommended contents? If not, what items must caregivers add? _____

_____

_____

Part IV: Apply What You Have Learned

1. Describe an appropriate attendance policy for ill children in your center._____

_____

_____

_____

_____

_____

_____

2. Describe how you would arrange for an isolation area in your child care center. _____

_____

_____

_____

_____

_____

_____

Copyright Goodheart-Willcox Co., Inc.

Apply What You Have Learned (Cont.)

3. Describe what you would do if a child in your care:

    A. fell and scraped a knee _____

    _____

    B. was hit in the head by a swing _____

    _____

    C. was stung by a bee _____

    _____

4. How should a center protect against head lice? _____

    _____

    _____

    _____

    _____

    _____

    _____

Copyright Goodheart-Willcox Co., Inc.

Developing Guidance Skills

■ Competency Goals:

■ To advance physical and intellectual competence
■ To support social and emotional development and provide positive guidance

■ Functional Areas:

■ Communication
■ Self
■ Social
■ Guidance

Part I: Read from *Working with Young Children*

■ Chapter 13
■ Appendix, *Mastering CDA Competencies*, Suggestions for Talking with a Child

Part II: Review What You Have Read

Directions: Answer the following questions.

1. What is the long-term goal of guidance? _____

_____

_____

2. Explain the difference between direct and indirect guidance. _____

_____

_____

_____

3. When setting limits, why is using simple language important? _____

_____

_____

_____

4. How can you encourage independence and cooperation in children? _____

_____

_____

_____

(Continued)

Copyright Goodheart-Willcox Co., Inc.

Review What You Have Read (Cont.)

5. List occasions when caregivers should intervene in children's activities. _____

_____

_____

_____

6. Give an example of indirect guidance. _____

_____

_____

7. What is time out and when might caregivers use it? _____

_____

_____

_____

8. Define and give an example of effective praise. _____

_____

_____

_____

9. Define and give an example of redirection. _____

_____

_____

_____

10. What is the best way to set an example for children? _____

_____

11. Describe how to ignore inappropriate behavior. _____

_____

_____

_____

12. Describe how a teacher can promote the development of self-concept in children. _____

_____

_____

_____

_____

Copyright Goodheart-Willcox Co., Inc.

Part III: Observe What You Have Learned

Observation A: Child Guidance Principles

■ Objectives

After completing this activity, you will be able to
■ describe various direct guidance principles
■ identify techniques for using direct guidance principles

■ Preparation

1. Observe a group of children in a classroom setting for a minimum of one hour.

2. Review the direct guidance principles listed on the chart that follows.

■ Setting

Place where observation occurred _____

_____

Phone number _____

Time _____ to _____

Name of caregiver_____

Title _____

Number of children present _____ Ages of children _____

■ The Observation

Observe a group of children for a minimum of one hour. Record examples of caregivers applying the direct guidance principles.

Guidance Principles	Examples Observed
1. Use simple language.	
2. Speak in a relaxed voice.	
3. Be positive.	
4. Offer choices with care.	
5. Encourage independence and cooperation.	
6. Be firm.	
7. Be consistent.	
8. Provide time for change.	
9. Consider feelings.	
10. Intervene when necessary.	

■ Review What You Have Observed

1. During your observation, what guidance principles did the caregiver use most frequently? Evaluate the effectiveness of each. _____

_____

_____

_____

_____

_____

_____

_____

_____

_____

Observation B: Physical and Verbal Guidance

■ Objectives

After completing this activity, you will be able to
- identify incidents of physical and verbal guidance
- observe how various direct guidance techniques affect individual children

■ Preparation

1. Arrange to observe children in a child care center, preschool, Head Start, kindergarten, or family child care home.

2. Review physical and verbal guidance in your text.

3. Review the chart that follows.

■ Setting

Place where observation occurred _____

_____

Phone number _____ Time _____ to _____

Name of caregiver_____

Title _____

Number of children present _____ Ages of children _____

Copyright Goodheart-Willcox Co., Inc.

■ The Observation

Observe children with their caregivers. On the chart below, record incidents of verbal and physical guidance you observe. Types of physical guidance include holding, touching, nudging, etc. Note how the incidents affect children's behavior.

	Type of Verbal Guidance	Type of Physical Guidance	Effect on Child
Description of incident			
Description of incident			
Description of incident			
Description of incident			
Description of incident			
Description of incident			

■ Review What You Have Observed

1. List examples of caregivers providing positive verbal guidance. _____

_____

_____

_____

_____

2. List examples of caregivers providing positive physical guidance. _____

_____

_____

_____

_____

_____

(Continued)

Copyright Goodheart-Willcox Co., Inc.

3. Describe instances during which the caregiver used verbal and physical guidance to encourage independence.

_____

_____

_____

_____

_____

_____

4. List an instance the caregiver modeled positive behavior and a child copied it. _____

_____

_____

_____

_____

_____

_____

Observation C: Effective Guidance Techniques

■ Objectives

After completing this activity, you will be able to
- describe various effective guidance techniques
- identify techniques for effective guidance

■ Preparation

1. Arrange to observe a group of children in a classroom setting for a minimum of one hour.

2. Review the techniques for effective guidance on the chart that follows.

■ Setting

Place where observation occurred _____

_____

Phone number _____ Time _____ to _____

Name of caregiver_____

Title _____

Number of children present _____ Ages of children _____

   Copyright Goodheart-Willcox Co., Inc.

■ The Observation

Observe a group of children for a minimum of one hour. Record examples of caregivers applying the effective guide techniques.

Guidance Techniques	Examples Observed
1. Positive reinforcement	
2. Natural or artificial consequences	
3. Warning	
4. Time out	
5. I-messages	
6. Effective praise	
7. Suggesting	
8. Prompting	
9. Persuading	
10. Redirecting	
11. Modeling	
12. Listening	
13. Ignoring	
14. Encouraging	

■ Review What You Have Observed

1. During your observation, what guidance techniques did the caregiver use most frequently? Evaluate the effectiveness of each.

_____

_____

_____

_____

Observation D: Evaluating Self-Concept

■ Objectives

After completing this activity, you will be able to

- ■ identify a child's self-concept
- ■ evaluate a child's self-concept in the classroom setting
- ■ explain how an adult can influence a child's self-concept

■ Preparation

1. Arrange to observe a child in a child care setting.

2. Review the self-concept questions on the chart below.

■ Setting

Place where observation occurred _____

_____

Name of caregiver _____

Title _____

Age of child _____

■ The Observation

As you observe the child, answer the questions on the chart.

	Yes	No	Sometimes
1. Does the child speak positively about himself or herself?			
2. Does the child appear to feel proud of his or her appearance?			
3. Does the child appear to feel proud of his or her accomplishments?			
4. Does the child seem to accept failure?			
5. Is the child willing to try new experiences?			
6. Does the child make decisions independently?			
7. Does the child act independently?			
8. Does the child share his or her possessions?			
9. Is the child willing to vocalize thoughts?			
10. Is the child naturally curious?			
11. Does the child usually appear calm and controlled?			

Copyright Goodheart-Willcox Co., Inc.

■ Review What You Have Observed

1. Do you feel this child has a good self-concept? Explain. _____
   _____
   _____
   _____
   _____

2. How might the caregiver have promoted the child's self-concept? _____
   _____
   _____
   _____

3. How might the caregiver help children develop a sense of security? _____
   _____
   _____
   _____
   _____

Part IV: Apply What You Have Learned

1. Explain why it is important for caregivers to resist talking amongst themselves while working with children.
   _____
   _____
   _____

2. Describe how you would help children understand and talk about their feelings. ____
   _____
   _____
   _____
   _____
   _____

3. In order to properly supervise children, where is the best place for a caregiver to stand in the classroom? Why?
   _____
   _____
   _____

(Continued)

Copyright Goodheart-Willcox Co., Inc.

4. Describe an occasion when you or a caregiver you have observed warned a child. Was the warning effective? If not, how would you handle the situation differently? _____

_____

_____

_____

_____

_____

_____

5. Complete the following caregiver checklist for promoting a positive self-concept.

	Yes	No	Sometimes
1. Do I observe children carefully before speaking?			
2. Am I an open-minded person?			
3. Do I recognize and value differences in children?			
4. Do I constantly strive to gain more knowledge about the world and share it with the children?			
5. Do I provide the children with choices so they may become independent deicision makers?			
6. Am I constantly trying to increase my human relations skills?			
7. Do I state directions in a positive manner?			
8. Do I encourage parents to share their attitudes with me?			
9. Do I avoid showing favoritism?			
10. Do I listen to the children?			
11. Do I help children sort out their mixed emotions?			
12. Do I plan developmentally appropriate activities?			
13. Do I respect cultural differences in children?			
14. Do I permit enough time to complete activities?			
15. Do I call attention to positive interactions between and among children?			
16. Do I make expectations clear?			
17. Do I acknowledge the child's attempts at tasks as well as accomplishments?			
18. Do I encourage children to use self-statements of confidence?			

Copyright Goodheart-Willcox Co., Inc.

Guidance Problems

■ Competency Goal:

■ To support social and emotional development and provide positive guidance

■ Functional Areas:

■ Guidance
■ Communication

■ Part I: Read from *Working with Young Children*

■ Chapter 14

■ Part II: Review What You Have Read

Directions: Answer the following questions.

1. List some causes of behavior problems in children. _____

_____

_____

_____

_____

2. What causes children to become overstimulated? _____

_____

_____

_____

3. How might you control children's frustrations? _____

_____

_____

_____

_____

4. What symptoms might indicate that medication is causing a child's behavior problems? _____

_____

_____

_____

(Continued)

Copyright Goodheart-Willcox Co., Inc.

5. How might caregivers involve onlookers in classroom activities? _____

_____

_____

_____

_____

6. If Anita lacks appetite, cries often, and kicks other children, how might you determine whether she is suffering from stress? _____

_____

_____

_____

_____

7. Compare ways two-year-olds and four-year-olds express anger. _____

_____

_____

_____

_____

8. How might caregivers stop children from biting others? _____

_____

_____

_____

_____

9. How can attending a child care program help curb thumbsucking for some children? _____

_____

_____

_____

10. How might caregivers help children conquer their fears? _____

_____

_____

_____

Copyright Goodheart-Willcox Co., Inc.

Part III: Observe What You Have Learned

Observation A: Possible Signs of Stress

■ Objectives

After completing this activity, you will be able to
- ■ identify possible signs of stress in children
- ■ describe incidents in an early childhood setting that involve stressors

■ Preparation

1. Arrange to observe children in a classroom setting for a minimum of one hour.
2. Review the following list of stressors.

■ Setting

Place where observation occurred _____

_____

Time _____ to _____

Name of caregiver_____

Title _____

Number of children present _____ Ages of children _____

■ The Observation

As you observe, record the names of children and stressors you suspect, then describe each incident.

Stressors

accident-proneness	eating problems	kicking
anger	excessive aggressiveness	nightmares
anxiety	excessive laziness	pounding heart
baby talk	fingernail biting	respiratory tract illness
bed wetting	headaches	stuttering
biting	hitting	tattling
crying spells	indigestion	teeth grinding
detachment	insomnia	temper tantrums
disinterest	irritability	thumbsucking

Child	Stressor	Description of Incident

■ Review What You Have Observed

1. Describe the classroom situation that caused most children stress. _____

   _____

   _____

   _____

   _____

   _____

2. During the situation described above, compare the similarities and differences between the stressors children exhibited. _____

   _____

   _____

   _____

   _____

   _____

   _____

3. Overall, how did the caregiver's actions and disposition promote a positive environment to help reduce stress? _____

   _____

   _____

   _____

   _____

   _____

   _____

Observation B: Handling Guidance Problems

■ Objectives

After completing this activity, you will be able to

■ identify incidents of children's anger, fear, and overstimulation in the classroom
■ identify ways to handle these guidance problems with children

■ Preparation

1. Arrange to observe children in a classroom setting.

2. Review the following guidance problems.

Copyright Goodheart-Willcox Co., Inc.

■ Setting

Place where observation occurred _____

_____

Phone number _____

Time _____ to _____

Name of caregiver_____

Title _____

Number of children present _____ Ages of children _____

■ The Observation

Record your observations of children with the following guidance problems.

1. Describe two instances of children showing anger. How did the caregiver handle each situation?

Instance A._____

_____

_____

_____

_____

_____

_____

_____

_____

_____

_____

Instance B._____

_____

_____

_____

_____

_____

_____

_____

_____

_____

_____

_____

2. Describe two instances in which children experienced fear. How did the caregiver handle each situation?

Instance A. _____

_____

_____

_____

_____

_____

Instance B. _____

_____

_____

_____

_____

_____

3. Describe two instances in which overstimulation caused disruptive behaviors. How did the caregiver handle each situation?

Instance A. _____

_____

_____

_____

_____

_____

Instance B. _____

_____

_____

_____

_____

_____

Copyright Goodheart-Willcox Co., Inc.

■ Review What You Have Observed

1. Describe alternative ways the caregiver might have guided the children's anger. _____

_____

_____

_____

_____

_____

2. Based on your observations, describe how understanding a fearful child's personality helped the caregiver to guide him or her. _____

_____

_____

_____

_____

_____

3. Describe how group size affected an instance you observed of overstimulation. Could the situation have been avoided? Explain. _____

_____

_____

_____

_____

_____

4. Did the caregiver model positive, appropriate behavior? Explain. _____

_____

_____

_____

_____

5. Did the caregiver give attention to positive behavior? Explain. _____

_____

_____

_____

_____

Copyright Goodheart-Willcox Co., Inc.

Part IV: Apply What You Have Learned

1. Describe a childhood fear you experienced. What helped you overcome it? _____

_____

_____

_____

_____

_____

2. Describe how you would help a child who bites other children. _____

_____

_____

_____

_____

_____

3. Compare how an 18-month-old and a three-year-old might express anger. _____

_____

_____

_____

_____

_____

4. How might you cut down on waiting times to help children behave properly? _____

_____

_____

_____

_____

5. How can you help an aggressive child to behave? _____

_____

_____

_____

_____

_____

Copyright Goodheart-Willcox Co., Inc.

Establishing Classroom Limits

■ Competency Goals:

■ To establish and maintain a safe, healthy learning environment
■ To support social and emotional development and provide positive guidance

■ Functional Areas:

■ Safe
■ Self
■ Social
■ Guidance

Part I: Read from *Working with Young Children*

■ Chapter 15

Part II: Review What You Have Read

Directions: Answer the following questions.

1. List three reasons for establishing classroom limits. _____

_____

_____

_____

2. Rewrite the following limits so they are short, simple, and positive.

   Don't stand on the swing. _____

   _____

   Don't leave scissors on the floor._____

   _____

   Don't leave paint spills on the table. _____

   _____

   Don't run indoors. _____

   _____

   Don't tear pages of books. _____

   _____

3. Why are flexible limits important in classrooms? _____

_____

_____

_____

(Continued)

Copyright Goodheart-Willcox Co., Inc.

4. How does your reaction to children who violate limits affect other children?_____
_____
_____
_____
_____
_____

5. List two examples of limits for the sensory play area. _____
_____
_____
_____

6. What concepts might cooking activities teach? _____
_____
_____
_____

7. Why should blockbuilding activities be allowed only during a set time period?_____
_____
_____
_____

8. How can you encourage children to explore the book corner? _____
_____
_____
_____
_____

9. Why aren't swings found on all playgrounds? _____
_____
_____
_____

10. What limits might be established for using seesaws?_____
_____
_____
_____
_____
_____

Copyright Goodheart-Willcox Co., Inc.

Part III: Observe What You Have Learned

Observation A: Observing Classroom Limits

■ Objectives

After completing this activity, you will be able to

■ explain how limits protect children's health and safety
■ explain how limits help children explore more freely
■ describe how to set simple, positive limits children understand
■ recognize methods caregivers use to enforce classroom limits

■ Preparation

1. Arrange to visit a child care center, preschool, or kindergarten.

2. Before the visit, obtain a copy of the classroom limits and goals. If unavailable in written form, ask the director or caregiver to verbally share them.

3. Record each limit on the chart.

■ Setting

Place where observation occurred _____

_____

Phone number _____

Time _____ to _____

Name of caregiver_____

Title _____

Number of children present _____ Ages of children _____

■ The Observation

Observe children and staff, keeping classroom limits in mind. Complete the chart below as you observe. List one example of how each limit is enforced.

Limits	Caregiver Behavior
Children clean spills.	Mrs. Green handed Barry a towel to wipe spilled milk.

(Continued)

Limits	Caregiver Behavior

■ Review What You Have Observed

1. Recall two classroom limits and give examples of how they reflect the center's goals. _____

_____

_____

_____

_____

2. Choose three classroom limits and explain how their enforcement protects children's health and safety. _____

_____

_____

_____

_____

_____

_____

3. Choose three limits and explain how their enforcement helps children to explore more freely. _____

_____

_____

_____

_____

_____

_____

(Continued)

Copyright Goodheart-Willcox Co., Inc.

Review What You Have Observed (Cont.)

4. List an example of a limit that was easy for children to understand and a limit that was more difficult.

   Easy _____

   _____

   Difficult _____

   _____

5. Were children less likely to follow limits they did not understand? Explain. _____

   _____

   _____

   _____

   _____

Observation B: Enforcing Limits

■ Objectives

After completing this activity, you will be able to

- identify ways children violate classroom limits
- identify appropriate methods caregivers can use to enforce limits
- recognize the need for flexible classroom limits

■ Preparation

1. Arrange to visit a child care center, preschool, or kindergarten.

2. Before the visit, obtain a copy of the classroom limits and goals. If unavailable in written form, ask the director or caregiver to verbally share them.

■ Setting

Place where observation occurred _____

_____

Phone number _____

Time _____ to _____

Name of caregiver _____

Title _____

Date _____

Number of children present _____ Ages of children _____

■ The Observation

Observe children and staff, keeping classroom limits in mind. Complete the chart below as you observe. Record examples of broken limits, caregiver responses, and whether you agree or disagree with each response. If you disagree with the caregiver's response, list an alternative response.

Limit violated _____

Caregiver response _____

_____

_____

Alternative response _____

_____

_____

Limit violated _____

Caregiver response _____

_____

_____

Alternative response _____

_____

_____

Limit violated _____

Caregiver response _____

_____

_____

Alternative response _____

_____

_____

Limit violated _____

Caregiver response _____

_____

_____

Alternative response _____

_____

_____

Copyright Goodheart-Willcox Co., Inc.

■ Review What You Have Observed

1. Based on your observations, list several guidelines for enforcing limits. _____

_____

_____

_____

_____

_____

_____

_____

_____

2. Explain why children follow limits best in a fairly consistent environment. _____

_____

_____

_____

_____

_____

_____

_____

_____

3. Did the caregiver adapt limits to the needs of an immediate situation? Describe the situation. _____

_____

_____

_____

_____

_____

_____

_____

_____

Copyright Goodheart-Willcox Co., Inc.

Part IV: Apply What You Have Learned

1. Every classroom area needs limits. Write possible limits for the areas listed below. Refer to your text if you need help.

Sensory play _____

_____

Dramatic play _____

_____

Cooking _____

_____

Music _____

_____

Art _____

_____

Book corner _____

_____

Blockbuilding _____

_____

Science _____

_____

Playground _____

_____

Small manipulative _____

_____

Technology _____

_____

Writing _____

_____

Play yard _____

_____

2. List methods caregivers can use to remind children of existing limits. _____

_____

_____

_____

_____

Copyright Goodheart-Willcox Co., Inc.

Handling Daily Routines

■ Competency Goals:

■ To establish and maintain a safe, healthy learning environment
■ To support social and emotional development and provide positive guidance

■ Functional Areas:

■ Learning Environment
■ Physical
■ Cognitive
■ Healthy
■ Guidance

Part I: Read from *Working with Young Children*

■ Chapter 16

Part II: Review What You Have Read

Directions: Answer the following questions.

1. Why are routines important for children?_____

_____

_____

_____

2. How might caregivers label lockers or cubbies so three-year-olds recognize their own? _____

_____

3. Describe one way to demonstrate how to tie shoes._____

_____

_____

_____

4. What factors influence children's appetites? _____

_____

_____

_____

5. How can you help three-year-olds learn to set the table?_____

_____

_____

(Continued)

Copyright Goodheart-Willcox Co., Inc.

6. At what age do eating problems usually peak? _____

_____

_____

7. How can you encourage children who refuse to eat? _____

_____

_____

_____

8. How can you discourage children from dawdling with their food? _____

_____

_____

_____

_____

_____

9. Describe rituals that might help children settle down at nap time. _____

_____

_____

_____

_____

10. List and describe the four basic methods for making transitions. _____

_____

_____

_____

_____

_____

_____

_____

_____

Copyright Goodheart-Willcox Co., Inc.

Part III: Observe What You Have Learned

Observation A: Classroom Routines

■ Objectives

After completing this activity, you will be able to
- ■ list effective ways to handle classroom routines
- ■ describe children's reactions to routines

Preparation

1. Arrange to observe children in a preschool, child care, or Head Start setting. Discuss your objectives with the contact person, then choose a time to observe the routines listed.

Setting

Place where observation occurred _____

_____

Name of caregiver _____

Title _____

Number of children present _____ Ages of children _____

The Observation

Observe the following routine situations. Record the caregiver's statements and actions as well as the children's reactions.

Routine	Caregiver's Statements and Actions	Children's Reactions
Dressing and undressing		
Toileting		
Eating		
Napping		

Review What You Have Observed

1. Based on your observations, give three suggestions for introducing routines. _____

_____

_____

_____

_____

_____

2. Describe other ways the caregiver might have handled routines listed on the chart. _____

_____

_____

_____

_____

_____

Observation B: Limits for Eating

■ Objectives

After completing this activity, you will be able to
- ■ identify limits for eating
- ■ describe methods the caregiver used to encourage independence
- ■ describe children's reactions to limits for eating

■ Preparation

1. Arrange to observe children in an early childhood program as they eat a snack, breakfast, or lunch.

2. Review the limits for eating listed on the observation form.

■ Setting

Place where observation occurred _____

_____

Time _____ to _____

Name of caregiver_____

Title _____

Number of children present _____ Ages of children _____

Copyright Goodheart-Willcox Co., Inc.

■ The Observation

Observe the caregiver and children during mealtime. Describe observations related to each eating limit.

Limits	Observation
Children help to set tables.	
Children serve themselves and learn appropriate table behavior.	
Children help with cleanup and clear own places when ready.	
Children are offered finger foods. They use child-sized plates, cups, and utensils. Caregivers encourage toddlers to use spoons.	
Children are to wipe their own spills without adult supervision. Children and caregivers engage in conversation during mealtime.	
Children are not required to finish food on their plate in order to receive dessert. However, children are exposed to many foods. Food is not used as a reward or punishment.	

Copyright Goodheart-Willcox Co., Inc.

■ Review What You Have Observed

1. In your observation, how effectively did caregivers enforce the limits for eating listed on the chart? Explain.

_____

_____

_____

_____

_____

_____

_____

_____

_____

_____

2. How did the caregiver encourage independence as children ate? _____

_____

_____

_____

_____

_____

_____

_____

_____

Part IV: Apply What You Have Learned

1. For each of the following methods for making transitions, provide at least one example you would use.

A. Concrete _____

_____

B. Visual _____

_____

C. Novelty _____

_____

D. Auditory _____

_____

(Continued)

Copyright Goodheart-Willcox Co., Inc.

Apply What You Have Learned (Cont.)

2. Evaluate the daily schedule in your classroom by answering the following questions.

A. Is the schedule dependable yet flexible to meet children's needs? Explain. _____

_____

_____

_____

B. Are there times for children to self-select activities? Explain. _____

_____

_____

_____

C. Is an adult available as a resource? Explain. _____

_____

_____

_____

D. Are there small group activities? Are they developmentally appropriate? Explain._____

_____

_____

_____

E. Are activities adapted to meet individual needs and special needs of children with disabilities? Explain.

_____

_____

_____

F. Are quiet and active activities alternated? Explain. _____

_____

_____

_____

G. Is cleanup time scheduled? Do children help maintain the setting by picking up toys? Explain.

_____

_____

_____

H. Are there provisions for toileting and hand washing? Describe. _____

_____

_____

_____

(Continued)

Copyright Goodheart-Willcox Co., Inc.

I. Are there provisions for indoor and outdoor activities? Explain. _____

_____

_____

_____

J. Do caregivers offer children opportunities to develop their senses? Explain. _____

_____

_____

_____

K. Do caregivers use well-timed input to help children think about their experiences? Explain.

_____

_____

_____

3. Evaluate the effectiveness of your center in handling daily routines. What areas need improvement?

_____

_____

_____

_____

_____

_____

_____

_____

_____

_____

_____

Copyright Goodheart-Willcox Co., Inc.

The Curriculum

■ Competency Goals:

■ To advance physical and intellectual competence
■ To ensure a well-run, purposeful program responsive to participant needs

■ Functional Areas:

■ Physical
■ Cognitive
■ Communication
■ Creative
■ Social
■ Program Management

Part I: Read from *Working with Young Children*

■ Chapter 17

Part II: Review What You Have Read

Directions: Answer the following questions.

1. Define program goals. _____

_____

_____

_____

2. Who is involved in curriculum development? _____

_____

_____

_____

_____

_____

_____

_____

_____

_____

(Continued)

Copyright Goodheart-Willcox Co., Inc.

Review What You Have Read (Cont.)

3. Contrast direct and indirect learning experiences. _____

_____

_____

_____

_____

4. What three questions help caregivers plan the curriculum? _____

_____

_____

_____

5. How do the learning styles of field-sensitive and field-independent children differ from each other? _____

_____

_____

_____

_____

_____

_____

6. Why are themes used in curriculum planning? _____

_____

_____

_____

7. How do block plans and lesson plans differ? _____

_____

_____

_____

_____

8. List the three parts of learning objectives. _____

_____

_____

_____

9. Define the term *motivation.* _____

_____

_____

(Continued)

Copyright Goodheart-Willcox Co., Inc.

Review What You Have Read (Cont.)

10. Describe the difference between the terms *closure* and *transition* as they relate to lesson plans. _____

_____

_____

Part III: Observe What You Have Learned

Observation A: Learning Styles

■ Objectives

After completing this activity, you will be able to
■ identify children's learning styles
■ describe teaching methods that suit various learning styles

■ Preparation

1. Arrange to observe five children in a child care setting.

2. Discuss the children's names, ages, and probable learning styles with the caregiver. Record the information below.

3. Review the text material on learning styles.

■ Setting

Place where observation occurred _____

_____

Name of caregiver_____

Title _____

First names, ages, and probable learning styles of children

1. _____ Age _____ Learning style _____

2. _____ Age _____ Learning style _____

3. _____ Age _____ Learning style _____

4. _____ Age _____ Learning style _____

5. _____ Age _____ Learning style _____

■ The Observation

As you observe the children, record actions or words that reveal their learning styles. Next, record effective teaching methods the caregiver used to suit these learning styles.

Child	Actions/Words that Reveal Learning Style	Teaching Methods

■ Review What You Have Observed

1. Do your observations confirm the caregiver's assessment of each child's learning style? Explain.

_____

_____

_____

_____

_____

_____

_____

_____

_____

2. Did the teaching methods suit each child's learning style? Explain. _____

_____

_____

_____

_____

_____

_____

_____

_____

_____

Copyright Goodheart-Willcox Co., Inc.

Observation B: Themes in the Classroom

■ Objectives

After completing this activity, you will be able to
- explain theme development as used by an early childhood caregiver
- identify theme-related objects and activities in a classroom

■ Preparation

1. Arrange to visit a child care center, preschool, kindergarten, or Head Start program. Choose a time when the caregiver can speak with you for about 15 minutes.

2. Review the questions below.

■ Setting

Place where observation occurred _____

_____

Name of caregiver_____

Title _____

Ages of children in center_____

■ The Observation

Ask the caregiver the questions below, then record his or her answers.

1. How do you select classroom themes? _____

   _____

   _____

   _____

2. How do you develop activities and materials to complement themes? _____

   _____

   _____

   _____

3. How do you make the curriculum and theme unbiased regarding sex, race, and special needs? Explain. ____

   _____

   _____

4. What is today's theme? _____

5. How long has this theme been used? _____

   _____

   _____

(Continued)

Copyright Goodheart-Willcox Co., Inc.

The Observation (Cont.)

Observe the classroom for about one hour. Record examples of objects and activities that relate to the day's theme.

Theme-Related Objects	Theme-Related Activities

■ Review What You Have Observed

1. List some of the activity's developmental goals. Describe how theme-related objects and activities complemented these goals. _____

_____

_____

_____

_____

_____

_____

_____

_____

_____

_____

_____

Part IV: Apply What You Have Learned

1. For each area below, list activities you might use to support a classroom theme focusing on dogs.

Art _____

_____

Fingerplays _____

_____

Foods _____

_____

Math _____

_____

(Continued)

Copyright Goodheart-Willcox Co., Inc.

Music _____

_____

Science _____

_____

Sensory table _____

_____

Socio-dramatic play _____

_____

Storytelling _____

_____

Technology _____

_____

Writing _____

_____

2. List activities you might use to support a classroom theme focusing on telephones.

Art _____

_____

Fingerplays _____

_____

Foods _____

_____

Math _____

_____

Music _____

_____

Science _____

_____

Sensory table _____

_____

Socio-dramatic play _____

_____

Storytelling _____

_____

(Continued)

Copyright Goodheart-Willcox Co., Inc.

Apply What You Have Learned (Cont.)

Technology _____

_____

Writing_____

_____

3. Choose one activity about dogs and one activity about telephones, then write a transition to move children from one activity to the other. _____

_____

_____

_____

_____

_____

_____

_____

4. Write a learning objective for each of the two activities used above.

Dog Activity _____

_____

_____

_____

_____

_____

_____

_____

Telephone Activity _____

_____

_____

_____

_____

_____

_____

_____

Copyright Goodheart-Willcox Co., Inc.

Chapter 18

Guiding Art, Blockbuilding, and Sensory Experiences

■ Competency Goal:

■ To advance physical and intellectual competence

■ Functional Areas:

■ Physical
■ Cognitive
■ Communication
■ Creative

Part I: Read from *Working with Young Children*

■ Chapter 18

Part II: Review What You Have Read

Directions: Answer the following questions.

1. How does art promote physical development? _____

_____

_____

_____

2. How does art promote emotional growth? _____

_____

_____

3. How can you help children during the scribbles stage? _____

_____

_____

_____

4. Compare how children understand art in the scribbles and basic forms stages. _____

_____

_____

_____

_____

(Continued)

5. Describe the first drawings often created by children. _____

_____

_____

6. To reduce costs, what ingredient can caregivers add to powdered tempera paint? _____

7. List the benefits of using newsprint. _____

_____

_____

_____

8. How does fingerpainting promote children's development? _____

_____

_____

9. Compare how two-year-olds and four-year-olds handle play dough. _____

_____

_____

_____

10. How does making collages promote development? _____

_____

_____

_____

11. Describe how blockbuilding promotes learning in the four developmental domains. _____

_____

_____

_____

_____

_____

_____

12. What are the benefits from the sensory experiences of sand and water play? _____

_____

_____

_____

(Continued)

Copyright Goodheart-Willcox Co., Inc.

Part III: Observe What You Have Learned

Observation A: Learning Through Art Experiences

■ Objective

After completing this activity, you will be able to
■ describe what children learn by participating in art experiences

■ Preparation

1. Arrange to visit a child care center during an art activity.
2. Review the chart that follows.

■ Setting

Place where observation occurred _____

_____

Name of caregiver_____

Title _____

Number of children present _____ Ages of children _____

Art activity observed_____

■ The Observation

As you observe the art activity, record how the children learn the skills listed below. In the next column, note what the children do or say that implies they are learning these skills.

Learning Through Art	Notes on Learning
Express feelings.	
Value and respect the artwork of self and others.	
Discover new ways to use materials. Using materials in unconventional ways accepted.	
Use a variety of equipment and tools.	
Mix materials.	
Become aware of color, line, texture, and form.	
Use creativity.	

■ Review What You Have Observed

1. What were the most valuable learning aspects of the art activity?

_____

_____

2. Did the children appear to enjoy the art activity? Explain. _____

_____

_____

Observation B: Evaluating an Art Activity

■ Objective

After completing this activity, you will be able to

■ evaluate an art activity, the children's responses, and the caregiver's strategies

■ Preparation

1. Arrange to visit a child care center during an art activity.

2. Review the questions listed below.

■ Setting

Place where observation occurred _____

_____

Name of caregiver_____

Title _____

Art activity observed_____

■ The Observation

■ To evaluate the art activity, answer the questions below as you observe.

I. The Activity

A. Is the content worth knowing? Why or why not? _____

_____

_____

B. Was the activity developmentally appropriate? Explain. _____

_____

_____

(Continued)

Copyright Goodheart-Willcox Co., Inc.

The Observation (Cont.)

C. Did it interest children? Explain. _____

_____

_____

_____

_____

D. Did it include opportunities for children to test their knowledge? Explain. _____

_____

_____

_____

_____

II. The Children's Responses

A. Did all children reach the learning objective? If not, why? _____

_____

_____

_____

_____

B. Were there behavior problems? If so, what might have caused them? _____

_____

_____

_____

_____

III. The Caregiver's Strategies

A. Was the caregiver well organized? Explain. _____

_____

_____

_____

_____

_____

(Continued)

Copyright Goodheart-Willcox Co., Inc.

The Observation (Cont.)

B. Did the caregiver use effective teaching strategies to help children reach the learning objective? Give examples.

_____

_____

_____

_____

_____

C. Did the caregiver introduce concepts in a stimulating manner? Give examples. _____

_____

_____

_____

_____

_____

D. Did the caregiver effectively guide or manage the group? Explain. _____

_____

_____

_____

_____

_____

E. Were the children involved in the activity's closure? How? _____

_____

_____

_____

_____

_____

F. What teaching strategies should be changed if this activity is repeated? _____

_____

_____

_____

_____

_____

(Continued)

Copyright Goodheart-Willcox Co., Inc.

The Observation (Cont.)

G. Did the caregiver communicate frequently with each child individually? Explain._____

_____

_____

_____

_____

_____

■ Review What You Have Observed

1. Compare the completed activities of two children you observed. How did their finished products reflect their levels of development? _____

_____

_____

_____

_____

_____

_____

_____

_____

2. How did the caregiver reduce the cost of the art activity? Explain._____

_____

_____

_____

_____

3. Did the caregiver make art materials available daily to older toddlers and preschoolers for independent use? How did the availability of materials affect children's art activities? _____

_____

_____

_____

_____

_____

_____

(Continued)

Copyright Goodheart-Willcox Co., Inc.

4. Did the caregiver offer a variety of art materials as children become developmentally ready? How did developmentally appropriate materials affect children? _____

_____

_____

_____

Part IV: Apply What You Have Learned

1. Describe the art of a two-year-old you have observed. What stage would you consider this child's work?___

_____

_____

_____

_____

2. Compare the art of a three-year-old and a five-year-old you have observed. What stage or stages would you consider their work? _____

_____

_____

_____

_____

3. Describe how the caregiver in a classroom you have observed stored art supplies. Are improvements needed? Explain. _____

_____

_____

_____

4. Compare a three-year-old's and five-year-old's activities with play dough. _____

_____

_____

_____

_____

5. Describe art projects you have observed. What skills were the children learning? _____

_____

_____

_____

_____

Copyright Goodheart-Willcox Co., Inc.

Guiding Storytelling Experiences

■ **Competency Goal:**

■ To advance physical and intellectual competence

■ **Functional Areas:**

■ Physical
■ Cognitive
■ Communication
■ Creative

Part I: Read from *Working with Young Children*

■ Chapter 19

Part II: Review What You Have Read

Directions: Answer the following questions.

1. List six advantages of storytelling. _____

_____

_____

_____

_____

_____

_____

2. List and describe the five types of children's books. _____

_____

_____

_____

_____

_____

_____

_____

_____

_____

_____

(Continued)

Review What You Have Read (Cont.)

3. What are the criteria for illustrations? _____

_____

_____

_____

_____

4. How long will a two-year-old remain interested in a book? How long will a five-year-old remain interested?

_____

_____

5. What should caregivers consider when selecting books for infants? _____

_____

_____

_____

_____

6. What types of stories do four-year-olds enjoy? _____

_____

_____

_____

_____

7. List and explain stereotypes to avoid when selecting books. _____

_____

_____

_____

_____

8. Describe how to begin stories. _____

_____

_____

_____

9. Describe a draw-and-tell story. _____

_____

_____

10. What is a flannel board story? _____

_____

_____

Copyright Goodheart-Willcox Co., Inc.

Part III: Observe What You Have Learned

Observation A: Illustrations and Storytelling

■ Objectives

After completing this activity, you will be able to
■ select children's books that feature excellent illustrations
■ identify children's reactions to illustrations

■ Preparation

1. Select three children's books to share with children.

2. Arrange to read the books to children.

■ Setting

Place where observation occurred _____

_____

Number of children present _____

Ages of children _____

■ The Observation

Observe children as you read the three books, then evaluate their reactions to the stories on the chart below.

Books	Children's Reactions
Book name _____ Author _____ Illustrator _____ Publisher _____ Publication date _____	
Book name _____ Author _____ Illustrator _____ Publisher _____ Publication date _____	
Book name _____ Author _____ Illustrator _____ Publisher _____ Publication date _____	

■ Review What You Have Observed

1. Describe the criteria you used to select the books. _____
   _____
   _____
   _____
   _____

2. Did children react to the illustrations as you expected? Explain. _____
   _____
   _____
   _____
   _____
   _____

3. What have you learned about choosing books with excellent illustrations? _____
   _____
   _____
   _____
   _____
   _____

Observation B: Evaluating a Storytelling Activity

■ Objective

After completing this activity, you will be able to
- ■ evaluate a storytelling activity, the children's responses, and the caregiver's strategies

■ Preparation

1. Arrange to observe a storytelling activity in a child care setting.
2. Review the questions that follow.

■ Setting

Place where observation occurred _____

_____

Name of caregiver _____

Title _____

Activity observed _____

Copyright Goodheart-Willcox Co., Inc.

■ The Observation

Evaluate the activity you observe by answering the questions below.

I. The Activity

A. Is the content worth knowing? Why or why not? _____

_____

_____

_____

_____

_____

B. Was the activity developmentally appropriate? Explain. _____

_____

_____

_____

_____

_____

C. Did the story interest children? Explain. _____

_____

_____

_____

_____

_____

D. Did the activity include opportunities for the children to test their knowledge? Explain. _____

_____

_____

_____

_____

_____

II. The Children's Responses

A. Did all children reach the learning objective? If not, why? _____

_____

_____

_____

_____

_____

(Continued)

Copyright Goodheart-Willcox Co., Inc.

The Observation (Cont.)

B. Were there behavior problems? If so, what do you think might have caused them? _____

_____

_____

_____

_____

_____

III. The Caregiver's Strategies

A. Was the caregiver well organized? Explain. _____

_____

_____

_____

_____

B. Did the caregiver use effective teaching strategies to help children reach the learning objective? Give examples.

_____

_____

_____

_____

_____

C. Did the caregiver introduce concepts in a stimulating manner? Give examples. _____

_____

_____

_____

_____

_____

D. Did the caregiver effectively guide or manage the group? Explain. _____

_____

_____

_____

_____

_____

(Continued)

Copyright Goodheart-Willcox Co., Inc.

The Observation (Cont.)

E. Did the caregiver give children the opportunity to write as they showed interest? Explain. _____

_____

_____

_____

_____

F. Were the children involved in the activity's closure? How? _____

_____

_____

_____

_____

G. What teaching strategies should be changed if this activity is repeated? _____

_____

_____

_____

_____

■ Review What You Have Observed

1. How did the caregiver introduce the story? Was this an effective method? Why or why not? _____

_____

_____

_____

_____

2. Describe the relationships between the children and storyteller during the activity. _____

_____

_____

_____

_____

3. From your observations, what are some favorite poems of children? Explain why they are so well liked.

_____

_____

_____

_____

_____

(Continued)

Copyright Goodheart-Willcox Co., Inc.

4. Were the children active participants instead of passive listeners? Explain. _____

_____

_____

_____

_____

Part IV: Apply What You Have Learned

1. List children's books that deal with the topics of reproduction, separation, divorce, remarriage, and family diversity. _____

_____

_____

_____

2. List children's books that support the development of sexual identity. _____

_____

_____

_____

3. Choose a book and critique its illustrations based on the criteria listed in your text. _____

_____

_____

_____

4. Describe attractive and effective book displays in your classroom or in a classroom you have observed.

_____

_____

_____

5. Critique the storytelling of a caregiver you have observed based on the criteria listed in your text.

_____

_____

_____

6. Read a story aloud to a group of children. Critique your performance._____

_____

_____

_____

   Copyright Goodheart-Willcox Co., Inc.

Chapter 20

Guiding Play and Puppetry Experiences

■ **Competency Goal:**

■ To advance physical and intellectual competence

■ **Functional Areas:**

■ Physical
■ Cognitive
■ Communication
■ Creative

Part I: Read from *Working with Young Children*

■ Chapter 20

Part II: Review What You Have Read

Directions: Answer the following questions.

1. Describe the difference between dramatic play and socio-dramatic play. _____

   _____

   _____

   _____

2. Describe how socio-dramatic play promotes physical, social, emotional, and cognitive development.

   _____

   _____

   _____

   _____

   _____

   _____

3. What is cooperative play? Compare it to parallel play. _____

   _____

   _____

   _____

4. Define and give an example of personification. _____

   _____

   _____

(Continued)

Copyright Goodheart-Willcox Co., Inc.

5. Compare the manipulative and functional stages of material use. _____

_____

_____

_____

_____

6. What are the play themes of four-year-olds? _____

_____

_____

_____

7. Describe the difference between coaching and modeling. _____

_____

_____

_____

8. What type of areas promote more socio-dramatic play? _____

_____

9. What is a prop box? _____

_____

10. Describe a "me" puppet. _____

_____

_____

_____

_____

Part III: Observe What You Have Learned

Observation A: Socio-Dramatic Play

■ Objectives

After completing this activity, you will be able to

■ describe the materials and equipment used for socio-dramatic play
■ discuss the caregiver's role in supporting socio-dramatic play

Copyright Goodheart-Willcox Co., Inc.

■ Preparation

1. Arrange to observe the socio-dramatic play activities of a group of children, ages three through five, in a child care setting.

2. Review the questions that follow.

■ Setting

Place where observation occurred _____

_____

Name of caregiver _____

Title _____

Number of children present _____

Ages of children _____

■ The Observation

1. Describe the socio-dramatic play area. _____

_____

_____

_____

_____

_____

_____

_____

_____

_____

_____

_____

_____

2. List equipment in the dramatic play area. _____

_____

_____

_____

_____

_____

_____

_____

_____

The Observation (Cont.)

3. Describe the different types of play you observe. _____

_____

_____

_____

_____

_____

_____

_____

4. Describe the caregiver's role. _____

_____

_____

_____

_____

_____

_____

_____

■ Review What You Have Observed

1. Is the classroom's socio-dramatic play area located where it should be in the classroom? Why or why not?

_____

_____

_____

2. List six other materials that could be added to the dramatic play area. _____

_____

_____

_____

_____

_____

3. Did the caregiver encourage and respect children's choices of play? Explain. _____

_____

_____

_____

Copyright Goodheart-Willcox Co., Inc.

Observation B: Evaluating a Socio-Dramatic Play Activity and Caregiver Responsibilities

■ Objective

After completing this activity, you will be able to

■ evaluate a socio-dramatic play activity, the children's responses, and the caregiver's strategies

■ Preparation

1. Arrange to observe a socio-dramatic play activity in a child care setting.

2. Review the questions that follow.

■ Setting

Place where observation occurred _____

_____

Name of caregiver_____

Title _____

Activity observed _____

■ The Observation

■ Evaluate the activity you observe by answering the questions that follow.

I. The Activity

A. Is the content worth knowing? Why or why not? _____

_____

_____

_____

_____

B. Was the activity developmentally appropriate? Explain. _____

_____

_____

_____

_____

_____

C. Did it interest children? Explain._____

_____

_____

_____

_____

(Continued)

Copyright Goodheart-Willcox Co., Inc.

The Observation (Cont.)

    D. Did it include opportunities for children to test their knowledge? Explain. _____

_____

_____

_____

_____

_____

_____

II. The Children's Responses

    A. Did all children reach the learning objective? If not, why? _____

_____

_____

_____

_____

_____

    B. Were there behavior problems? If so, what do you think might have caused them? _____

_____

_____

_____

_____

_____

III. The Caregiver's Strategies

    A. Was the caregiver well organized? Explain. _____

_____

_____

_____

_____

    B. Did the caregiver use effective teaching strategies to help children reach the learning objective? Give examples.

_____

_____

_____

_____

_____

(Continued)

Copyright Goodheart-Willcox Co., Inc.

The Observation (Cont.)

C. Did the caregiver introduce concepts in a stimulating manner? Give examples. _____

_____

_____

_____

_____

_____

D. Did the caregiver effectively guide or manage the group? Did the caregiver encourage creativity?
Explain. _____

_____

_____

_____

_____

E. Were children involved in the activity's closure? How?_____

_____

_____

_____

_____

_____

F. What teaching strategies should be changed if this activity is repeated? _____

_____

_____

_____

_____

Review What You Have Observed

1. Describe a physical, social, emotional, and cognitive skill you observed a child developing. In what socio-dramatic play activity was the child engaged?

Physical skill _____

Play activity_____

_____

_____

Social skill _____

Play activity _____

_____

_____

Copyright Goodheart-Willcox Co., Inc.

Emotional skill _____

Play activity _____

_____

_____

Cognitive skill _____

Play activity _____

_____

_____

2. How did scheduling affect children's socio-dramatic play activities? Explain. _____

_____

_____

_____

_____

_____

_____

_____

3. How did the variety of props available affect children's play? _____

_____

_____

_____

_____

_____

_____

_____

Part IV: Apply What You Have Learned

1. Describe an example of parallel play you have observed. _____

_____

_____

_____

_____

_____

_____

(Continued)

Copyright Goodheart-Willcox Co., Inc.

Apply What You Have Learned (Cont.)

2. Describe an example of cooperative play you have observed. _____

_____

_____

_____

_____

_____

3. Describe an example of the functional stage of material use you have observed. Compare this with an example of the manipulative stage you have observed. _____

_____

_____

_____

_____

_____

_____

_____

_____

_____

_____

_____

4. Describe an example of three-year-olds' play themes you have observed. _____

_____

_____

_____

_____

_____

5. Provide an example of five-year-olds' play themes you have observed. _____

_____

_____

_____

_____

_____

(Continued)

Copyright Goodheart-Willcox Co., Inc.

Apply What You Have Learned (Cont.)

6. Provide an example you have observed of a caregiver coaching a child. _____

_____

_____

_____

_____

_____

_____

7. Reread the chapter's puppet information, then write a puppet story below or on a separate sheet. Begin with a theme and develop a plot.

_____

_____

_____

_____

_____

_____

_____

_____

_____

_____

_____

_____

_____

_____

_____

_____

_____

_____

_____

_____

Copyright Goodheart-Willcox Co., Inc.

Guiding Manuscript Writing Experiences

■ **Competency Goal:**

■ To advance physical and intellectual competence

■ **Functional Areas:**

■ Physical
■ Cognitive
■ Communication

Part I: Read from *Working with Young Children*

■ Chapter 21

Part II: Review What You Have Read

Directions: Answer the following questions.

1. How does manuscript writing differ from cursive writing? _____

_____

_____

_____

_____

2. List at least six reasons to encourage writing in preschool. _____

_____

_____

_____

_____

_____

_____

3. What elements are needed to help children meet writing objectives? _____

_____

_____

_____

4. What two skills do children need before they can use manuscript writing? _____

_____

_____

(Continued)

Copyright Goodheart-Willcox Co., Inc.

Review What You Have Read (Cont.)

5. List materials used to promote fine motor development. _____
_____
_____
_____

6. List at least three activities that improve hand-eye coordination. _____
_____
_____
_____

7. In what sequence do children learn alphabet letters? _____
_____
_____
_____
_____
_____

8. What might cause wavering lines in children's writing? _____
_____
_____
_____
_____

9. Describe how to determine a child's preferred writing hand. _____
_____
_____
_____
_____

10. What is skywriting? _____
_____
_____
_____
_____

Copyright Goodheart-Willcox Co., Inc.

Part III: Observe What You Have Learned

Observation A: Children's Writing Skills

■ Objectives

After completing this activity, you will be able to

- identify methods of teaching writing skills in an early childhood environment
- list examples of how caregivers use manuscript writing in the classroom
- compare the handwriting skills of four- and five-year-olds
- discuss the caregiver's role in calling attention to writing skills

■ Preparation

1. Arrange to visit a child care center, family child care home, preschool, Head Start, or kindergarten program during an activity that involves writing skills.

2. Review the questions that follow.

■ Setting

Place where observation occurred _____

_____

Name of caregiver _____

Title _____

Number of children present _____

Ages of children _____

■ The Observation

As you observe, write responses to the questions that follow.

1. List examples of how children use writing skills in the classroom. _____

_____

_____

_____

_____

_____

_____

_____

_____

_____

(Continued)

Copyright Goodheart-Willcox Co., Inc.

2. Compare the children's writing abilities. _____

_____

_____

_____

_____

_____

3. List examples of the caregiver's use of writing skills in the classroom. _____

_____

_____

_____

_____

_____

_____

4. What materials encourage writing in the classroom setting? _____

_____

_____

_____

_____

_____

_____

■ Review What You Have Observed

1. Why is it important that caregivers have good handwriting skills? _____

_____

_____

_____

_____

2. What materials could be added to encourage the children's interest in writing? _____

_____

_____

_____

_____

Copyright Goodheart-Willcox Co., Inc.

Observation B: Evaluating a Prewriting or Handwriting Activity

■ Objective

After completing this activity, you will be able to

■ evaluate a prewriting or handwriting activity, the children's responses, and the caregiver's strategies

■ Preparation

1. Arrange to observe a prewriting or handwriting activity in a child care setting.

2. Review the questions that follow.

■ Setting

Place where observation occurred _____

_____

Name of caregiver_____

Title _____

Activity observed _____

■ The Observation

■ As you observe, evaluate the handwriting activity by answering the questions that follow.

I. The Activity

A. Is the skill worth developing? Why or why not? _____

_____

_____

_____

_____

B. Was the activity developmentally appropriate? Explain. _____

_____

_____

_____

_____

_____

C. Did it interest children? Explain._____

_____

_____

_____

_____

_____

(Continued)

Copyright Goodheart-Willcox Co., Inc.

The Observation (Cont.)

D. Did it include opportunities for children to test their knowledge? Explain. _____

_____

_____

_____

_____

_____

II. The Children's Responses

A. Did all children reach the learning objective? If not, why? _____

_____

_____

_____

_____

_____

B. Were there behavior problems? If so, what do you think might have caused them? _____

_____

_____

_____

_____

_____

III. The Caregiver's Strategies

A. Was the caregiver well organized? Explain. _____

_____

_____

_____

_____

_____

B. Did the caregiver use effective teaching strategies to help children reach the learning objective? Give examples.

_____

_____

_____

_____

_____

(Continued)

Copyright Goodheart-Willcox Co., Inc.

The Observation (Cont.)

C. Did the caregiver introduce concepts in a stimulating manner? Give examples. _____

_____

_____

_____

_____

_____

D. Did the caregiver effectively guide or manage the group? Explain. _____

_____

_____

_____

_____

_____

E. Were children involved in the activity's closure? How? _____

_____

_____

_____

_____

_____

F. What teaching strategies should be changed if this activity is repeated? _____

_____

_____

_____

_____

_____

■ Review What You Have Observed

1. Were writing materials developmentally appropriate? Explain. _____

_____

_____

_____

Part IV: Apply What You Have Learned

1. In a classroom you have observed, describe the space designated to promote writing. Is it suitable? Explain.

_____

_____

_____

_____

_____

_____

2. Describe methods you (or a caregiver you have observed) have used to promote writing. _____

_____

_____

_____

_____

_____

_____

_____

_____

_____

3. Describe the writing abilities of a four-year-old versus a five-year-old you have observed. _____

_____

_____

_____

_____

_____

_____

_____

_____

4. Describe problems you have observed in children's writing. _____

_____

_____

_____

_____

_____

Copyright Goodheart-Willcox Co., Inc.

Chapter 22

Guiding Math Experiences

■ **Competency Goal:**

■ To advance physical and intellectual competence

■ **Functional Area:**

■ Cognitive

Part I: Read From *Working with Young Children*

■ Chapter 22

Part II: Review What You Have Read

Directions: Answer the following questions.

1. Describe the two ways to assess children's math abilities. _____

_____

_____

_____

_____

_____

2. Why is color considered a math concept? _____

_____

_____

_____

3. Define *shape*. _____

_____

4. Describe why matching and sorting are classification tasks. _____

_____

_____

_____

_____

_____

5. What concept must children understand before they can learn to add and subtract? _____

_____

(Continued)

6. Describe the difference between rote and rational counting. _____

   _____

   _____

   _____

7. Provide at least three examples of words given in the text that stress space concepts. _____

   _____

   _____

   _____

8. Provide at least three examples of words given in the text that help children understand time concepts.

   _____

   _____

   _____

Part III: Observe What You Have Learned

Observation A: Classroom Areas and Math Concepts

■ Objectives

After completing this activity, you will be able to
- ■ observe mathematical learning in the classroom
- ■ cite experiences in a classroom activity area that help children develop math concepts
- ■ discuss math concepts involved in a classroom activity area

■ Preparation

1. Review the text information on math concepts and activities.

■ Setting

Place where observation occurred _____

_____

Name of caregiver _____

Title _____

Number of children present _____ Ages of children _____

Activity observed _____

Copyright Goodheart-Willcox Co., Inc.

■ The Observation

Choose an activity area to observe, such as art, science, music, etc. As you observe, record play experiences that promote math skills. Also record concepts the math experiences help form, such as color, shape, classification, sets, counting, numeral identification, space, size, volume, time, and temperature.

Concepts	Math Experiences

■ Review What You Have Observed

1. List examples of mathematical language the caregiver used to promote math skills. _____

   _____

   _____

   _____

2. List classroom equipment that fostered mathematical thinking. Describe how. _____

   _____

   _____

   _____

   _____

Observation B: Evaluating a Math Activity

■ Objective:

After completing this activity you will be able to

■ evaluate a math activity, the children's responses, and the caregiver's strategies

■ Preparation

1. Arrange to observe a math activity in a child care setting.

2. Review the questions that follow.

Copyright Goodheart-Willcox Co., Inc.

■ Setting

Place where observation occurred _____

_____

Name of caregiver _____

Title _____

Activity observed _____

■ The Observation

As you observe, evaluate the activity by answering the questions that follow.

I. The Activity

A. Is the content worth knowing? Why or why not? _____

_____

_____

B. Was the activity developmentally appropriate? Explain._____

_____

_____

C. Did it interest children? Explain._____

_____

_____

D. Did it include opportunities for children to test their knowledge? Explain._____

_____

_____

_____

II. The Children's Responses

A. Did all children reach the learning objective? If not, why? _____

_____

_____

_____

_____

B. Were there behavior problems? If so, what do you think might have caused them? _____

_____

_____

_____

_____

Copyright Goodheart-Willcox Co., Inc.

III. The Caregiver's Strategies

A. Was the caregiver well organized? Explain. _____

_____

_____

_____

B. Did the caregiver use effective teaching strategies to help children reach the learning objective? Give examples.

_____

_____

_____

_____

C. Did the caregiver introduce concepts in a stimulating manner? Give examples. _____

_____

_____

_____

_____

D. Did the caregiver effectively guide or manage the group? Explain. _____

_____

_____

_____

_____

E. Were children involved in the activity's closure? How? _____

_____

_____

_____

_____

F. What teaching strategies should be changed if this activity is repeated? _____

_____

_____

_____

_____

■ Review What You Have Observed

1. What equipment did the caregiver use? How might additional equipment have complemented the activity?

_____

_____

_____

_____

2. What math language did the caregiver use during the activity? How would you complement or change this language? _____

_____

_____

_____

_____

Part IV: Apply What You Have Learned

1. Describe how you might teach children color concepts. _____

_____

_____

_____

_____

_____

_____

2. Describe how you might teach children shape concepts. _____

_____

_____

_____

_____

_____

_____

3. Describe how you might teach children classification. _____

_____

_____

_____

_____

_____

_____

(Continued)

Copyright Goodheart-Willcox Co., Inc.

Apply What You Have Learned (Cont.)

4. Describe how you might teach children the concept of sets. _____

_____

_____

_____

_____

_____

_____

_____

_____

5. Describe how you might teach children number concepts. _____

_____

_____

_____

_____

_____

_____

_____

_____

_____

_____

6. Describe how you might teach children space concepts. _____

_____

_____

_____

_____

_____

_____

_____

_____

_____

_____

(Continued)

Copyright Goodheart-Willcox Co., Inc.

Apply What You Have Learned (Cont.)

7. Describe how you might teach children time concepts. _____

_____

_____

_____

_____

_____

_____

_____

_____

_____

_____

Copyright Goodheart-Willcox Co., Inc.

Guiding Science Experiences

■ **Competency Goal:**

■ To advance physical and intellectual competence

■ **Functional Areas:**

■ Cognitive
■ Communication

Part I: Read from *Working with Young Children*

■ Chapter 23

Part II: Review What You Have Read

Directions: Answer the following questions.

1. Why should science involve a hands-on approach? _____

_____

_____

_____

2. Describe the best location for the classroom science area._____

_____

_____

_____

3. What factors must caregivers consider when selecting science area equipment and materials? _____

_____

_____

_____

4. List at least three of the five basic process skills science activities promote. _____

_____

_____

_____

_____

5. What is a feely box? _____

_____

_____

_____

(Continued)

Copyright Goodheart-Willcox Co., Inc.

6. List at least four concepts taught with water. _____
_____
_____
_____
_____

7. What concepts can children learn from science experiments involving food?_____
_____
_____
_____
_____

8. What concepts can children learn from planting seeds?_____
_____
_____
_____
_____

9. What concepts can children learn from using magnets? _____
_____
_____
_____
_____

10. List animals that make good classroom pets. _____
_____
_____

Part III: Observe What You Have Learned

Observation A: Evaluating a Science Activity

■ Objective

After completing this activity, you will be able to
■ evaluate a science activity, the children's responses, and the caregiver's strategies

■ Preparation

1. Arrange to observe a science activity in a child care setting.
2. Review the questions below.

Copyright Goodheart-Willcox Co., Inc.

■ Setting

Place where observation occurred _____

Name of caregiver _____

Title _____

Activity observed _____

■ The Observation

As you observe, evaluate the activity by answering the questions below.

I. The Activity

A. Is the content worth knowing? Why or why not? _____

_____

_____

_____

B. Was the activity developmentally appropriate? Explain. _____

_____

_____

_____

_____

C. Did it interest children? Explain. _____

_____

_____

_____

_____

D. Did it include opportunities for children to test their knowledge? Explain. _____

_____

_____

_____

_____

II. The Children's Responses

A. Did all children reach the learning objective? If not, why? _____

_____

_____

_____

_____

(Continued)

Copyright Goodheart-Willcox Co., Inc.

The Observation (Cont.)

B. Were there behavior problems? If so, what do you think might have caused them? _____

_____

_____

_____

_____

_____

III. The Caregiver's Strategies

A. Was the caregiver well organized? Explain. _____

_____

_____

_____

_____

_____

B. Did the caregiver use effective teaching strategies to help children reach the learning objective? Give examples.

_____

_____

_____

_____

_____

C. Did the caregiver introduce concepts in a stimulating manner? Give examples. _____

_____

_____

_____

_____

_____

D. Did the caregiver effectively guide or manage the group? Explain. _____

_____

_____

_____

_____

_____

(Continued)

Copyright Goodheart-Willcox Co., Inc.

The Observation (Cont.)

E. Were children involved in the activity's closure? How? _____

_____

_____

_____

_____

F. What teaching strategies should be changed if this activity is repeated? _____

_____

_____

_____

_____

▮ Review What You Have Observed

1. What science equipment did the caregiver use? Might additional equipment have improved the activity? Explain.

_____

_____

_____

_____

_____

_____

_____

_____

2. What language did the caregiver use to promote children's understanding of science? Could the caregiver have used additional language? Explain.

_____

_____

_____

_____

_____

_____

_____

_____

Observation B: Science Literature

■ Objectives

After completing this activity, you will be able to
- ■ review children's books for science concepts
- ■ select a book with science concepts, prepare to read a story, and read aloud to a child or several children
- ■ identify children's reactions

■ Preparation

1. Visit the library and find three books that contain science concepts, then read the books.

2. Arrange to read one book to a child or small group of children.

3. Practice reading the story aloud in front of a mirror.

■ Setting

Place where observation occurred _____

_____

Number of children present _____

Ages of children _____

■ The Observation

In the chart that follows, list the three books, authors, and science concepts the books promote. Then read the book you chose aloud to a group of children, observing their reactions.

Book Name and Author	Science Concepts

Copyright Goodheart-Willcox Co., Inc.

■ Review What You Have Observed

1. How did you introduce the book? _____

_____

_____

_____

_____

_____

_____

_____

_____

2. How did the children respond to the book? _____

_____

_____

_____

_____

_____

_____

_____

_____

3. During the activity, what conversation occurred that indicated children were learning science concepts?

_____

_____

_____

_____

_____

_____

_____

_____

_____

_____

_____

_____

(Continued)

Copyright Goodheart-Willcox Co., Inc.

Review What You Have Observed (Cont.)

4. How did you end the activity? Was it effective? _____

_____

_____

_____

_____

_____

_____

_____

_____

_____

_____

_____

Part IV: Apply What You Have Learned

1. Give five examples of open-ended questions you might use in the science area. _____

_____

_____

_____

_____

_____

2. Describe a science experience you might use to help children understand their senses. _____

_____

_____

_____

_____

_____

3. Describe how you might use color to teach science concepts. _____

_____

_____

_____

_____

_____

(Continued)

Copyright Goodheart-Willcox Co., Inc.

Apply What You Have Learned (Cont.)

4. How might you use water to teach science concepts? _____

_____

_____

_____

_____

_____

5. Describe how you might use food to teach science concepts. _____

_____

_____

_____

_____

_____

_____

6. How might you use the children's own bodies to teach them about science? _____

_____

_____

_____

_____

_____

7. Describe how you could use gardening to teach science concepts. _____

_____

_____

_____

_____

_____

8. How might you use air to teach science concepts?_____

_____

_____

_____

_____

_____

_____

(Continued)

Copyright Goodheart-Willcox Co., Inc.

Apply What You Have Learned (Cont.)

9. Describe how you could use magnets to teach science concepts. _____

_____

_____

_____

_____

_____

10. How might you use wheels to teach science concepts? _____

_____

_____

_____

_____

_____

11. List several science concepts you could introduce on a field trip. _____

_____

_____

_____

_____

12. How might you use animals to teach science concepts? _____

_____

_____

_____

_____

_____

13. Describe two ways you could teach children the importance of caring for the earth. _____

_____

_____

_____

_____

Copyright Goodheart-Willcox Co., Inc.

Chapter 24

Guiding Social Studies Experiences

■ Competency Goal:

■ To advance physical and intellectual competence

■ Functional Areas:

■ Cognitive
■ Communication
■ Self
■ Social

Part I: Read from *Working with Young Children*

■ Chapter 24

Part II: Review What You Have Read

Directions: Answer the following questions.

1. Describe the importance of social studies. _____

_____

_____

_____

_____

2. Why are daily observations important to the quality of social studies programs?_____

_____

_____

_____

_____

3. How can caregivers determine children's ability levels? _____

_____

_____

_____

_____

4. Describe incidental learnings._____

_____

_____

_____

_____

(Continued)

Copyright Goodheart-Willcox Co., Inc.

5. Why is evaluation a key part of planning a social studies curriculum? _____
   _____
   _____
   _____

6. What are *perceptions?* _____
   _____
   _____
   _____
   _____
   _____

7. Why is a multicultural perspective important in planning a social studies curriculum? _____
   _____
   _____
   _____
   _____
   _____

8. Define *stereotyping.* How does it differ from omission? _____
   _____
   _____
   _____
   _____
   _____

9. Why might children form negative stereotypes about the aged? _____
   _____
   _____
   _____

10. Define *ecology.* _____
    _____
    _____
    _____

Copyright Goodheart-Willcox Co., Inc.

Part III: Observe What You Have Learned

Evaluating a Social Studies Activity

■ Objective

After completing this activity, you will be able to

■ evaluate a social studies activity, the children's responses, and the caregiver's strategies

■ Preparation

1. Prepare to observe a social studies activity in a child care setting.

2. Review the questions that follow.

■ Setting

Place where observation occurred _____

_____

Name of caregiver _____

Title _____

Activity observed _____

■ The Observation

As you observe, evaluate the activity by answering the questions below.

I. The Activity

A. Is the content worth knowing? Why or why not? _____

_____

_____

_____

_____

B. Was the activity developmentally appropriate? Explain. _____

_____

_____

_____

_____

C. Did it interest children? Explain. _____

_____

_____

_____

_____

(Continued)

Copyright Goodheart-Willcox Co., Inc.

The Observation (Cont.)

    D. Did it include opportunities for children to test their knowledge? Explain. _____

_____

_____

_____

_____

_____

II. The Children's Responses

    A. Did all children reach the learning objective? If not, why? _____

_____

_____

_____

_____

_____

    B. Were there behavior problems? If so, what do you think might have caused them? _____

_____

_____

_____

_____

_____

III. The Caregiver's Strategies

    A. Was the caregiver well organized? Explain. _____

_____

_____

_____

_____

_____

    B. Did the caregiver use effective teaching strategies to help children reach the learning objective? Give examples.

_____

_____

_____

_____

_____

(Continued)

Copyright Goodheart-Willcox Co., Inc.

The Observation (Cont.)

C. Did the caregiver introduce concepts in a stimulating manner? Give examples. _____

_____

_____

_____

D. Did the caregiver effectively guide or manage the group? Explain. _____

_____

_____

_____

E. Were children involved in the activity's closure? How? _____

_____

_____

_____

F. What teaching strategies should be changed if this activity is repeated? _____

_____

_____

_____

_____

■ Review What You Have Observed

1. Describe the caregiver's use of themes or concepts. _____

_____

_____

_____

_____

_____

_____

_____

_____

_____

_____

(Continued)

Copyright Goodheart-Willcox Co., Inc.

2. How might the caregiver have further utilized themes and concepts during the activity? _____

_____

_____

_____

_____

_____

_____

_____

_____

_____

_____

_____

Part IV: Apply What You Have Learned

1. Describe two examples of incidental learning you have observed. _____

_____

_____

_____

_____

_____

_____

_____

_____

_____

_____

_____

_____

_____

_____

(Continued)

Copyright Goodheart-Willcox Co., Inc.

Apply What You Have Learned (Cont.)

2. Describe how you might incorporate multicultural activities in the classroom. _____

_____

_____

_____

_____

_____

_____

_____

_____

_____

_____

_____

_____

_____

3. Describe an ecology activity you might plan._____

_____

_____

_____

_____

_____

_____

_____

_____

_____

_____

_____

_____

_____

_____

_____

(Continued)

Copyright Goodheart-Willcox Co., Inc.

Apply What You Have Learned (Cont.)

4. Describe a classroom activity you might use to positively portray the aged. _____

_____

_____

_____

_____

_____

_____

_____

_____

_____

_____

_____

_____

_____

_____

_____

_____

_____

_____

_____

Copyright Goodheart-Willcox Co., Inc.

Guiding Food and Nutrition Experiences

■ Competency Goals:

■ To establish and maintain a safe, healthy learning environment
■ To establish positive and productive relationships with families

■ Functional Areas:

■ Healthy
■ Cognitive
■ Communication
■ Families

Part I: Read from *Working with Young Children*

■ Chapter 25

Part II: Review What You Have Read

Directions: Answer the following questions.

1. List at least four limits to promote happy, relaxed food experiences. _____

_____

_____

_____

_____

2. How can you share eating and nutritional information with parents? _____

_____

_____

_____

_____

3. List the advantages of cooking experiences._____

_____

_____

_____

_____

_____

4. What is the best number of children to participate in a cooking experience? _____

_____

(Continued)

Copyright Goodheart-Willcox Co., Inc.

5. How can caregivers improve children's eating habits? _____

_____

_____

_____

_____

6. What might caregivers do when children refuse food? _____

_____

_____

_____

_____

_____

7. What do children learn from setting the table? _____

_____

_____

_____

_____

Part III: Observe What You Have Learned

Observation A: Important Food Concepts

■ Objectives

After completing this activity, you will be able to
- ■ identify important food concepts, how the caregiver promotes them, and children's reactions during a classroom cooking activity
- ■ evaluate the cooking activity

■ Preparation

1. Arrange to observe a cooking activity in a preschool, child care, Head Start, or kindergarten setting.

2. Review important food concepts in the chart that follows.

■ Setting

Place where observation occurred _____

_____

Name of caregiver _____

Title _____

Number of children present _____ Ages of children _____

Copyright Goodheart-Willcox Co., Inc.

■ The Observation

As you observe, record caregiver actions or words that teach the food concepts listed on the chart. Record children's reactions to each lesson.

Food Concepts	Caregiver Actions or Words	Children's Reactions to Teaching
Understanding cleanliness and safety measures		
Following directions		
Understanding nutritional knowledge		
Using motor skills		
Understanding food sources		
Identifying foods and food groups		
Using all the senses		
Counting and measuring carefully		
Understanding basic chemical changes		
Using cooking equipment		
Understanding cooking processes		

■ Review What You Have Observed

1. What effective methods did the caregiver use to promote food concepts? Describe why they worked so well.

_____

_____

_____

2. Overall, did children react as you had expected? What factors influenced their reactions? _____

_____

_____

_____

Copyright Goodheart-Willcox Co., Inc.

Observation B: Evaluating a Cooking Activity

■ Objective

After completing this activity, you will be able to

■ evaluate a cooking activity, the children's responses, and the caregiver's strategies

■ Preparation

1. Observe a cooking activity in a child care setting.
2. Review the questions that follow.

■ Setting

Place where observation occurred _____

Name of caregiver _____

Title _____

Activity observed _____

■ The Observation

As you observe, evaluate the activity by answering the questions that follow.

I. The Activity

A. Is the content worth knowing? Why or why not? _____

_____

_____

_____

_____

_____

B. Was the activity developmentally appropriate? Explain. _____

_____

_____

_____

_____

_____

C. Did it interest children? Explain. _____

_____

_____

_____

_____

_____

(Continued)

Copyright Goodheart-Willcox Co., Inc.

The Observation (Cont.)

D. Did it include opportunities for children to test their knowledge? Explain. _____

_____

_____

_____

_____

E. Did the caregiver ask open-ended questions? Explain. _____

_____

_____

_____

_____

II. The Children's Responses

A. Did all children reach the learning objective? If not, why? _____

_____

_____

_____

_____

B. Were there behavior problems? If so, what do you think might have caused them? _____

_____

_____

_____

_____

III. The Caregiver's Strategies

A. Was the caregiver well organized? Explain. _____

_____

_____

_____

_____

_____

(Continued)

Copyright Goodheart-Willcox Co., Inc.

B. Did the caregiver use effective teaching strategies to help children reach the learning objective? Give examples.

_____

_____

_____

_____

_____

C. Did the caregiver introduce concepts in a stimulating manner? Give examples. _____

_____

_____

_____

_____

_____

D. Did the caregiver effectively guide or manage the group? Explain. _____

_____

_____

_____

_____

_____

E. Were children involved in the activity's closure? How? _____

_____

_____

_____

_____

F. What teaching strategies should be changed if this activity is repeated? _____

_____

_____

_____

_____

_____

Copyright Goodheart-Willcox Co., Inc.

■ Review What You Have Observed

1. How did the caregiver promote nutrition concepts during the food activity? _____

_____

_____

_____

_____

_____

_____

2. How did the caregiver use serving or cleanup experiences to promote independence? Explain. _____

_____

_____

_____

_____

_____

_____

_____

Part IV: Apply What You Have Learned

1. Describe how you might promote good eating habits in children. _____

_____

_____

_____

_____

_____

_____

_____

_____

_____

2. Write titles for five newsletter articles designed to help parents understand eating and nutrition.

_____

_____

_____

_____

_____

(Continued)

Copyright Goodheart-Willcox Co., Inc.

Apply What You Have Learned (Cont.)

3. Describe a successful cooking experience you have conducted or observed. Why was it successful?

_____

_____

_____

_____

_____

_____

_____

_____

_____

_____

Copyright Goodheart-Willcox Co., Inc.

Chapter 26
Guiding Music and Movement Experiences

■ **Competency Goal:**

■ To advance physical and intellectual competence

■ **Functional Areas:**

■ Physical
■ Cognitive
■ Communication
■ Creative

Part I: Read from *Working with Young Children*

■ Chapter 26

Part II: Review What You Have Read

Directions: Answer the following questions.

1. Describe how music experiences benefit children. _____

   _____

   _____

   _____

   _____

2. When singing with children under age three, why should caregivers avoid using instruments to accompany the children? _____

   _____

   _____

3. List characteristics of the best songs caregivers should note when selecting music for young children.

   _____

   _____

   _____

   _____

4. List and describe the three methods used to teach songs. _____

   _____

   _____

   _____

   _____

   _____

(Continued)

Copyright Goodheart-Willcox Co., Inc.

5. Why do some caregivers prefer an Autoharp® to a piano? _____

_____

_____

_____

6. How do rhythm instruments complement a singing experience? _____

_____

_____

_____

_____

_____

7. When should caregivers schedule music? _____

_____

_____

_____

_____

_____

8. Describe why listening is an important music activity. _____

_____

_____

_____

_____

9. What is a chant? _____

_____

_____

10. What are body percussion activities? _____

_____

_____

_____

Copyright Goodheart-Willcox Co., Inc.

Part III: Observe What You Have Learned

Observation A: Music Experiences

■ Objectives

After completing this activity, you will be able to
- ■ describe the words and actions of a music experience
- ■ describe the caregiver's role in the music experience

■ Preparation

1. Arrange to observe a music activity in a preschool, child care, Head Start, or kindergarten setting.

■ Setting

Place where observation occurred _____

_____

Name of caregiver _____

Title _____

Number of children present _____

Ages of children _____

Activity observed _____

■ The Observation

In the space provided, describe in detail the words and actions you observe during the music activity. Also describe the caregiver's role in the activity.

Words and Actions During the Activity	Description of Caregiver's Role

■ Review What You Have Observed

1. Did the words and actions promote developmental skills? Did they complement the activity? Explain.

_____

_____

_____

_____

_____

_____

_____

2. Did the caregiver influence the activity's success? Explain. _____

_____

_____

_____

_____

_____

_____

_____

_____

Observation B: Evaluating a Music Activity

■ Objective

After completing this activity, you will be able to
■ evaluate a music activity, the children's responses, and the caregiver's strategies

■ Preparation

1. Arrange to observe a music activity in a child care setting.

2. Review the questions that follow.

■ Setting

Place where observation occurred _____

_____

Name of caregiver _____

Title _____

Activity observed _____

Ages of children _____

Copyright Goodheart-Willcox Co., Inc.

■ The Observation

As you observe, evaluate the activity by answering the questions below.

I. The Activity

A. Is the content worth knowing? Why or why not? _____

_____

_____

_____

_____

B. Was the activity developmentally appropriate? Explain._____

_____

_____

_____

_____

C. Did it interest children? Was creativity during the musical experience encouraged? Explain.

_____

_____

_____

_____

D. Did it include opportunities for children to test their knowledge? Explain. _____

_____

_____

_____

_____

E. Were musical instruments that children play themselves accessible? Explain. _____

_____

_____

_____

_____

II. The Children's Responses

A. Did all children reach the learning objective? If not, why? _____

_____

_____

_____

_____

(Continued)

Copyright Goodheart-Willcox Co., Inc.

The Observation (Cont.)

B. Were there behavior problems? If so, what do you think might have caused them? _____

_____

_____

_____

_____

_____

III. The Caregiver's Strategies

A. Was the caregiver well organized? Explain. _____

_____

_____

_____

_____

_____

B. Did the caregiver use effective teaching strategies to help children reach the learning objective? Give examples.

_____

_____

_____

_____

_____

C. Did the caregiver introduce concepts in a stimulating manner? Give examples. _____

_____

_____

_____

_____

_____

D. Did the caregiver effectively guide or manage the group? Explain. _____

_____

_____

_____

_____

_____

(Continued)

Copyright Goodheart-Willcox Co., Inc.

The Observation (Cont.)

E. Were children involved in the activity's closure? How? _____

_____

_____

_____

_____

_____

F. What teaching strategies should be changed if this activity is repeated? _____

_____

_____

_____

_____

_____

■ Review What You Have Observed

1. Noting the text's criteria for selecting songs, evaluate songs used during the music activity. Were they fitting for young children? Explain.

_____

_____

_____

_____

_____

_____

_____

_____

_____

_____

_____

_____

_____

_____

(Continued)

Copyright Goodheart-Willcox Co., Inc.

2. What instruments did children use? Did the caregiver effectively introduce them to children? How did the instruments affect the activity? Explain.

_____

_____

_____

_____

_____

_____

_____

_____

_____

_____

_____

_____

_____

_____

_____

_____

_____

_____

_____

Part IV: Apply What You Have Learned

1. Create a song using a familiar melody, such as "Twinkle, Twinkle Little Star." Introduce the song to a small group of children. Describe the children's reactions and evaluate your presentation skills.

Song_____

_____

_____

_____

_____

_____

_____

(Continued)

Copyright Goodheart-Willcox Co., Inc.

Apply What You Have Learned (Cont.)

Children's reactions _____

_____

_____

_____

_____

_____

Evaluation _____

_____

_____

_____

_____

_____

2. Plan a musical activity to present at your center. Think about the activity's purpose, the introduction, proce-dures, and closure. Conduct the activity with a group of children, then evaluate it.

Purpose of activity _____

_____

_____

_____

_____

Introduction _____

_____

_____

_____

_____

_____

Procedures _____

_____

_____

_____

Closing _____

_____

_____

_____

Copyright Goodheart-Willcox Co., Inc.

Evaluation _____

_____

_____

_____

3. Describe a movement activity you might use in a child care setting. Specify the children's ages.

_____

_____

_____

_____

_____

_____

_____

_____

_____

_____

4. Describe a song you have taught or observed children learning. What method was used to teach the song? Was it effective? Explain. _____

_____

_____

_____

_____

_____

_____

_____

Copyright Goodheart-Willcox Co., Inc.

Guiding Field Trip Experiences

■ Competency Goal:

■ To advance physical and intellectual competence

■ Functional Areas:

■ Safe
■ Physical
■ Cognitive
■ Communication
■ Social

Part I: Read from *Working with Young Children*

■ Chapter 27

Part II: Review What You Have Read

Directions: Answer the following questions.

1. Why are field trips important? _____

_____

_____

_____

_____

2. What might be an appropriate first field trip for young children? _____

_____

_____

_____

3. When selecting field trip sites, what might caregivers consider?_____

_____

_____

_____

_____

4. Describe the purpose of a pretrip. _____

_____

_____

_____

_____

(Continued)

Copyright Goodheart-Willcox Co., Inc.

5. When planning field trips for young children, why should caregivers avoid crowds?_____
_____
_____

6. Why should caregivers schedule field trips for midmorning? _____
_____
_____
_____
_____
_____
_____

7. Describe why field trips should begin after a quiet activity. _____
_____
_____
_____

8. On what is a field trip's adult-child ratio based?_____
_____
_____
_____
_____

9. List the three common field trip limits. _____
_____
_____
_____

10. What activities should caregivers plan to follow field trips? _____
_____
_____
_____
_____

Copyright Goodheart-Willcox Co., Inc.

Part III: Observe What You Have Learned

Observation A: The Pretrip

■ Objectives

After completing this activity, you will be able to
- select a field trip site for a group of children
- arrange a pretrip to the site

■ Preparation

1. Choose a field trip site that suits the developmental levels and interests of young children.

2. Arrange a pretrip visit to the site.

3. Review the questions in the form below.

■ Setting

Pretrip site _____

_____

Contact person _____

Title _____

Date _____

■ The Observation

Evaluate the field trip site by answering the questions that follow.

I. Communicating with the Resource Person

1. Describe your goals. Record the conversation. _____

_____

_____

_____

_____

_____

2. Describe children's developmental levels. Record the conversation. _____

_____

_____

_____

_____

_____

(Continued)

Copyright Goodheart-Willcox Co., Inc.

Observe What You Have Learned (Cont.)

3. Describe the children's interests. Record the conversation. _____

_____

_____

_____

_____

4. Describe types of questions the children may ask. Record the conversation. _____

_____

_____

_____

_____

_____

II. Preparing Logistics

1. Where are the bathrooms located? _____

_____

_____

2. If a bus is used, where is parking located? _____

_____

_____

III. Evaluating the Site

1. What special learning opportunities did you observe? _____

_____

_____

_____

_____

_____

2. Are there any dangers involved? Explain. _____

_____

_____

_____

_____

_____

_____

(Continued)

Copyright Goodheart-Willcox Co., Inc.

Observe What You Have Learned (Cont.)

3. Would the experience be valuable for children? Explain. _____

_____

_____

_____

_____

_____

4. If costs are involved, is the trip the best use of your resources? Why or why not? _____

_____

_____

_____

_____

_____

_____

5. What time of day would be best to tour this site? Why? _____

_____

_____

_____

_____

_____

■ Review What You Have Observed

1. Based on the evaluation questions, conclude whether or not this field trip is suitable for your group of children. Justify your answer.

_____

_____

_____

_____

_____

_____

_____

_____

_____

_____

Copyright Goodheart-Willcox Co., Inc.

Observation B: Evaluating a Field Trip

■ Objective

After completing this activity, you will be able to

■ evaluate a field trip, the children's responses, and the caregiver's strategies

■ Preparation

1. Arrange to accompany a caregiver and children from a child care center, preschool, or kindergarten on a field trip.

2. Review the questions that follow.

■ Setting

Field trip site _____

_____

Time _____ to _____

Date _____

Number of children present_____

Ages of children _____

■ The Observation

Evaluate the field trip by answering the questions that follow.

I. The Activity

A. Is the content worth knowing? Why or why not? _____

_____

_____

_____

_____

_____

B. Was the activity developmentally appropriate? Explain._____

_____

_____

_____

_____

_____

_____

_____

(Continued)

Copyright Goodheart-Willcox Co., Inc.

The Observation (Cont.)

C. Did it interest children? Explain. _____

_____

_____

_____

_____

D. Did it include opportunities for children to test their knowledge? Explain. _____

_____

_____

_____

_____

_____

II. The Children's Responses

A. Did all children reach the learning objective? If not, why? _____

_____

_____

_____

_____

_____

B. Were there behavior problems? If so, what do you think might have caused them? _____

_____

_____

_____

_____

III. The Caregiver's Strategies

A. Was the caregiver well organized? Explain. _____

_____

_____

_____

_____

_____

(Continued)

Copyright Goodheart-Willcox Co., Inc.

The Observation (Cont.)

B. Did the caregiver use effective teaching strategies to help children reach the learning objective? Give examples.

_____

_____

_____

_____

C. Did the caregiver introduce concepts in a stimulating manner? Give examples. _____

_____

_____

_____

_____

_____

D. Did the caregiver encourage children to respect the environment and others?_____

_____

_____

_____

_____

E. Did the caregiver effectively guide or manage the group? Explain. _____

_____

_____

_____

_____

_____

F. Were children involved in the activity's closure? How? _____

_____

_____

_____

_____

_____

G. What teaching strategies should be changed if this activity is repeated? _____

_____

_____

_____

_____

_____

(Continued)

Copyright Goodheart-Willcox Co., Inc.

■ Review What You Have Observed

1. Describe two follow-up activities you would use after the field trip.

Follow-up activity A. _____

_____

_____

_____

_____

_____

_____

_____

Follow-up activity B. _____

_____

_____

_____

_____

_____

_____

_____

Part IV: Apply What You Have Learned

1. List 10 ideas for field trips children might enjoy in your community. Next to each field trip idea, note the theme to which it relates.

Field Trip	Related Theme
1.	
2.	
3.	
4.	
5.	
6.	
7.	
8.	
9.	
10.	

(Continued)

Copyright Goodheart-Willcox Co., Inc.

2. To enrich a field trip, caregivers must plan educational goals carefully. Study the goals for conducting a field trip to a service station, listed below. Then write your own goals for conducting field trips to the other locations listed.

Goals for Visiting a Service Station ■ Observe mechanics at work. ■ Learn about car care. ■ See how machinery works. ■ Introduce the vocabulary words *mechanic, gas pump, noise, hoist,* and *tow truck.*	**Goals for Visiting a Beauty Salon**
Goals for Visiting a Post Office	**Goals for Visiting a Fire Station**
Goals for Visiting a Bakery	**Goals for Visiting a Florist**
Goals for Visiting an Apple Orchard	**Goals for Visiting a Grocery Store**

Copyright Goodheart-Willcox Co., Inc.

Programs for Infants and Toddlers

■ Competency Goals:

- ■ To establish and maintain a safe, healthy learning environment
- ■ To advance physical and intellectual competence
- ■ To support social and emotional development and provide positive guidance

■ Functional Areas:

- ■ Safe
- ■ Healthy
- ■ Learning Environment
- ■ Physical
- ■ Cognitive
- ■ Communication
- ■ Creative
- ■ Self
- ■ Social
- ■ Guidance
- ■ Program Management

Part I: Read from *Working with Young Children*

- ■ Chapter 28

Part II: Review What You Have Read

Directions: Answer the following questions.

1. What five areas should be included in an infant's environment? _____
   _____
   _____
   _____
   _____
   _____

2. What five areas should be included in a toddler's environment? _____
   _____
   _____
   _____
   _____
   _____

3. Why must caregivers promptly meet the needs of infants and toddlers? _____
   _____
   _____
   _____

(Continued)

Copyright Goodheart-Willcox Co., Inc.

4. Why do infants cry? _____

_____

_____

_____

5. When infants experience separation anxiety, how can caregivers reassure parents? _____

_____

_____

_____

_____

6. Why is a diaper checking routine a useful policy to follow? _____

_____

_____

_____

7. What should caregivers consider when planning a nap time schedule? _____

_____

_____

_____

_____

8. What purpose do toys serve for children? _____

_____

_____

_____

_____

9. Define the term *overfamiliarity*. _____

_____

_____

_____

_____

10. In an infant and toddler program, what information should the daily record include? _____

_____

_____

_____

_____

Copyright Goodheart-Willcox Co., Inc.

Part III: Observe What You Have Learned

Observation A: Programs for Infants and Toddlers

■ Objectives

After completing this activity, you will be able to
- sketch the room arrangement of a toddler program on graph paper
- evaluate the use of space in the room

■ Preparation

1. Arrange to visit a child care center with a toddler program.

2. Read the information on infant and toddler space in your text.

3. You will need a ruler and pencil to draw the floor plan.

■ Setting

Place where observation occurred _____

_____

■ The Observation

Sketch the room arrangement on the graph paper provided.

(Continued)

Room Arrangement

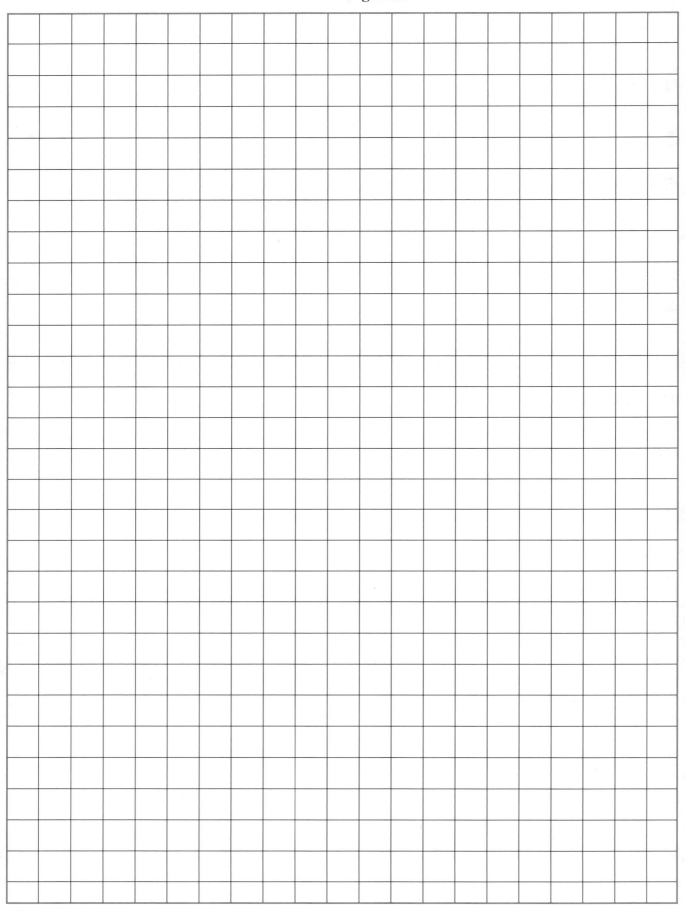

Copyright Goodheart-Willcox Co., Inc.

■ Review What You Have Learned

1. Describe each of the areas listed below.

Receiving area _____

_____

_____

_____

_____

Playing area _____

_____

_____

_____

_____

Napping area _____

_____

_____

_____

_____

Diapering area _____

_____

_____

_____

_____

Eating area _____

_____

_____

_____

_____

2. How would you improve the space? _____

_____

_____

_____

_____

_____

_____

_____

Observation B: Toy Inventory

■ Objectives

After completing this activity, you will be able to
- describe the environment of an infant/toddler program
- complete a toy inventory
- recommend additional program equipment

■ Preparation

1. Arrange to visit an infant/toddler classroom.

2. Review the toy categories on the chart below.

■ Setting

Place where observation occurred _____

■ The Observation

Record toys present in the center under the appropriate categories. Then list toys to add for each category.

Category	Toys Present	Toys to Add
Looking toys		
Reaching and grasping toys		
Cuddling toys		
Squeezing and manipulative toys		

(Continued)

Copyright Goodheart-Willcox Co., Inc.

The Observation (Cont.)

Category	Toys Present	Toys to Add
Kicking and hitting toys		
Pull/push toys		
Sound toys		
Gross-motor toys		
Fine-motor toys		

■ Review What You Have Observed

1. Evaluate the center's toy inventory. Does it provide children with a choice of interesting equipment? Are toys safe? How are they stored? How might caregivers expand the selection? _____

_____

_____

_____

_____

_____

_____

_____

_____

_____

_____

_____

Copyright Goodheart-Willcox Co., Inc.

Part IV: Apply What You Have Learned

1. What type of toys would you provide to promote gross motor skills? _____
   _____
   _____
   _____
   _____
   _____
   _____
   _____

2. What types of toys would you provide to promote fine motor skills? _____
   _____
   _____
   _____
   _____
   _____
   _____
   _____

3. Describe an activity file that you maintain or have observed. _____
   _____
   _____
   _____
   _____
   _____
   _____
   _____

4. Describe a sensory experience in which you have observed toddlers participate. Describe their reactions.
   _____
   _____
   _____
   _____
   _____
   _____
   _____
   _____

(Continued)

Copyright Goodheart-Willcox Co., Inc.

Programs for School-Age Children

■ Competency Goals:

- To establish and maintain a safe, healthy learning environment
- To advance physical and intellectual competency
- To support social and emotional development and provide positive guidance
- To ensure a well-run, purposeful program responsive to participants' needs

■ Functional Areas:

- Physical
- Cognitive
- Social
- Communication
- Creative
- Healthy
- Learning Environment
- Guidance
- Self

Part I: Read from *Working with Young Children*

- Chapter 29

Part II: Review What You Have Read

Directions: Answer the following questions.

1. Explain why school-age child care programs are important. _____

_____

_____

_____

_____

_____

2. List and describe the three different program models used as curriculum formats in school-age child care.

_____

_____

_____

_____

_____

_____

_____

_____

(Continued)

3. Why is it important to have appropriate adult-child ratios? _____

_____

_____

_____

_____

_____

_____

4. Who should care for school-age children? _____

_____

5. How can teachers in school-age programs promote respect for cultural diversity? _____

_____

_____

_____

_____

_____

_____

6. What activities would occur in the quiet area(s) of the classroom? _____

_____

_____

7. How does the teacher in a school-age program assess interests? _____

_____

_____

_____

_____

_____

_____

8. Explain how to conduct a group planning session. _____

_____

_____

_____

_____

_____

_____

(Continued)

Copyright Goodheart-Willcox Co., Inc.

9. How can mealtimes be learning experiences? _____

_____

_____

_____

_____

_____

_____

10. Why might children enjoy physical activities after sitting in a classroom all day? _____

_____

_____

_____

11. How do mixed-group activities benefit children?

_____

_____

_____

_____

Part III: Observe What You Have Learned

Quality School-Age Programs

■ Objectives

After completing this activity, you will be able to
- evaluate the quality of a school-age child care program
- recommend improvement for the school-age program observed

■ Preparation

1. Make arrangements to visit a school-age child care program.
2. Review the characteristics of a quality school-age program.

■ Setting

Place where observation occurred _____

_____

Address _____

Phone number _____

Contact person _____

Date _____

Time _____ to _____

Number of children _____

Other information _____

_____

_____

■ The Observation

As you observe the program, record evidence of how this program meets the characteristics of a quality school-age program.

Characteristics	Evidence
Appropriate adult-child ratios.	(Example: There was one caregiver for every eight children.)
Warm, caring, well-trained staff.	
Well-organized space with room for active play, quiet play, and interest centers.	
Curriculum based on children's emerging interests and needs.	
Appreciation of cultural diversity.	
Parent involvement to achieve shared goals for children.	

(Continued)

Copyright Goodheart-Willcox Co., Inc.

The Observation (Cont.)

Characteristics	Evidence
Flexible scheduling to allow for a balance of individual, small group, and large group activities.	
Appropriate and safe use of technology.	

■ Review What You Have Observed

1. Which characteristics of a quality school-age child care program were not observed? Explain. _____

_____

_____

_____

2. How would you rate the quality of this school-age program overall? _____

_____

_____

_____

3. What area(s) could be improved and what changes would you make? _____

_____

_____

_____

Part IV: Apply What You Have Learned

1. If you were setting up a quality school-age program, what equipment might you include in the interest centers that would promote the development of the skills listed below?

Math_____

_____

_____

Science_____

_____

_____

Social _____

_____

_____

(Continued)

Apply What You Have Learned (Cont.)

Emotional _____

_____

_____

Gross Motor_____

_____

_____

Fine Motor_____

_____

_____

Language Comprehension_____

_____

_____

Expressive Language_____

_____

_____

Writing _____

_____

_____

Technology _____

_____

_____

2. List the components you would include in a typical daily schedule in a school-age child care program. _____

_____

_____

_____

_____

_____

_____

_____

Copyright Goodheart-Willcox Co., Inc.

Guiding Children with Special Needs

■ Competency Goals:

■ To ensure a well-run, purposeful program responsive to participants' needs
■ To establish and maintain a safe, healthy learning environment

■ Functional Areas:

■ Learning Environment
■ Program Management

Part I: Read from *Working with Young Children*

■ Chapter 30

Part II: Review What You Have Read

Directions: Answer the following questions.

1. Define the term *inclusion*. _____

_____

_____

2. List the six components of an Individualized Education Plan. _____

_____

_____

_____

_____

_____

_____

3. What is the purpose of a hearing aid? What are its limitations? _____

_____

_____

4. What speaking conditions can caregivers create to help a stuttering child? _____

_____

_____

5. List common vision problems. _____

_____

_____

_____

(Continued)

Copyright Goodheart-Willcox Co., Inc.

6. What is a chronic health need? _____

_____

_____

7. If an epileptic child has a seizure, how can a caregiver help control the situation? _____

_____

_____

_____

_____

_____

_____

8. How can caregivers integrate children with special needs into the classroom? _____

_____

_____

_____

_____

_____

_____

9. List the six areas in which gifted children may possess exceptional skills. _____

_____

_____

_____

_____

_____

10. Define *acceleration*. _____

_____

_____

_____

Copyright Goodheart-Willcox Co., Inc.

Part III: Observe What You Have Learned

Observing a Special Needs Child

■ Objectives

After completing this activity, you will be able to
- describe the behavior of a special needs child in a classroom setting
- evaluate assistance given to the special needs child

■ Preparation

1. Arrange to observe a special needs child in a child care setting.

2. Discuss the child's special needs with the caregiver.

3. Review the text material on special needs children.

■ Setting

Place where observation occurred _____

_____

Name of caregiver_____

Title _____

First name _____

Age _____

Special needs of child_____

_____

■ The Observation

As you observe the special needs child, answer the questions below.

1. Describe the child's special needs. _____

_____

_____

_____

_____

2. Describe behaviors you observed that indicate the child may have special needs. _____

_____

_____

_____

_____

(Continued)

Copyright Goodheart-Willcox Co., Inc.

3. Describe activities the child was able to perform without assistance. _____

_____

_____

_____

4. Describe activities the child could not perform without assistance. _____

_____

_____

_____

5. Describe assistance the caregiver gave the child. _____

_____

_____

_____

6. Describe assistance other children gave the child. _____

_____

_____

_____

_____

_____

7. Did the child appear to be "labeled" by the caregiver or children? Explain your answer. _____

_____

_____

_____

_____

_____

■ Review What You Have Observed

1. Were the child's special needs satisfied? Justify your answer. _____

_____

_____

_____

_____

_____

_____

_____

_____

(Continued)

Copyright Goodheart-Willcox Co., Inc.

Review What You Have Observed (Cont.)

2. Describe additional assistance the caregiver and parents might give this child. _____

_____

_____

_____

_____

_____

_____

_____

3. Describe changes in the classroom's physical setting that might help the child. _____

_____

_____

_____

_____

_____

_____

_____

_____

Part IV: Apply What You Have Learned

1. Speak with a special needs teacher. Ask how he or she integrates special needs children into the classroom. Summarize his or her feedback below. _____

_____

_____

_____

_____

_____

_____

_____

_____

_____

_____

(Continued)

Copyright Goodheart-Willcox Co., Inc.

Apply What You Have Learned (Cont.)

2. How would you care for a child with allergies? _____

_____

_____

_____

_____

_____

3. Describe experiences you have encountered or observed with a child who has a vision disorder. _____

_____

_____

_____

_____

_____

4. How might observing and recording notes about children help caregivers offer successful daily programs?

_____

_____

_____

_____

_____

Copyright Goodheart-Willcox Co., Inc.

Parent Involvement

■ **Competency Goal:**

■ To establish positive and productive relationships with families

■ **Functional Area:**

■ Families

Part I: Read from *Working with Young Children*

■ Chapter 31

Part II: Review What You Have Read

Directions: Answer the following questions.

1. List four examples of parent involvement activities. _____

   _____

   _____

   _____

   _____

2. Describe the difference between a newsletter and a letter. _____

   _____

   _____

   _____

3. What points should caregivers remember about writing style? _____

   _____

   _____

   _____

4. List the types of information a newsletter may include. _____

   _____

   _____

   _____

   _____

5. What are the three phases of parent-teacher conferences? _____

   _____

   _____

   _____

(Continued)

6. Where should caregivers conduct parent-teacher conferences? _____

_____

_____

7. How can caregivers reassure worried parents? _____

_____

_____

8. What is the purpose of a discussion group? _____

_____

_____

_____

9. What is the purpose of a problem-solving file? _____

_____

_____

_____

10. What is a sunshine call? _____

_____

_____

_____

Part III: Observe What You Have Learned

Volunteer Orientation

■ Objective

After completing this activity, you will be able to
■ describe an orientation session for parent volunteers in an early childhood program

■ Preparation

1. Arrange to attend an orientation session for parent volunteers.
2. Review the following observation questions.

Copyright Goodheart-Willcox Co., Inc.

■ Setting

Place where observation occurred _____

_____

Name of caregiver_____

Title _____

Session observed_____

■ The Observation

As you observe the session, answer the following:

1. List the topics discussed during the orientation._____

   _____

   _____

   _____

   _____

   _____

2. List the types of information the caregiver shared with parents. _____

   _____

   _____

   _____

   _____

   _____

   _____

   _____

   _____

   _____

3. List four questions from parents and the caregiver's responses.

   A. Question _____

   _____

   Response _____

   _____

   _____

   B. Question _____

   _____

   Response _____

   _____

   _____

(Continued)

Copyright Goodheart-Willcox Co., Inc.

C. Question _____

_____

Response _____

_____

_____

D. Question _____

_____

Response _____

_____

_____

■ Review What You Have Observed

1. Describe the conference setting. How did the caregiver create a comfortable environment? How would you complement the setting?

_____

_____

_____

_____

2. How did the caregiver show he or she was listening as parents spoke? How did the caregiver show he or she appreciated the parents' involvement? _____

_____

_____

_____

_____

_____

Part IV: Apply What You Have Learned

1. For each area listed below, write the titles of three articles to appear in a newsletter you might send to parents.

A. Review of special activities

_____

_____

_____

(Continued)

Copyright Goodheart-Willcox Co., Inc.

Apply What You Have Learned (Cont.)

B. Upcoming events at the center

_____

_____

_____

C. Home activities for parents and children

_____

_____

_____

D. Child development information (may include recommended reading)

_____

_____

_____

E. Nutritious recipes

_____

_____

_____

F. Parent volunteer update (may include recognition and requests for volunteers)

_____

_____

_____

G. Meet the staff

_____

_____

_____

2. Describe a parent-teacher conference you have hosted or observed. List what you would repeat and what you would change about the meeting.

_____

_____

_____

_____

_____

_____

_____

_____

(Continued)

Copyright Goodheart-Willcox Co., Inc.

3. How might a caregiver help parents understand a child's development in order to meet the child's needs?

_____

_____

_____

_____

_____

4. Describe a sunshine call you have made or heard a caregiver make. _____

_____

_____

_____

_____

_____

_____

_____

5. How might a caregiver incorporate information about families' cultures, religions, and parenting practices into classroom experiences? _____

_____

_____

_____

_____

_____

Copyright Goodheart-Willcox Co., Inc.

A Career for You in Child Care

- ■ **Competency Goal:**
  - ■ To maintain a commitment to professionalism

- ■ **Functional Area:**
  - ■ Professionalism

Part I: Read from *Working with Young Children*

- ■ Chapter 32

Part II: Review What You Have Read

Directions: Answer the following questions.

1. What is a resume? _____

   _____

   _____

2. List the purposes of a resume. _____

   _____

   _____

   _____

   _____

3. Why should candidates specify the month and year of each job's starting and ending date? _____

   _____

   _____

   _____

4. Describe why placing a newspaper ad is considered a passive job search technique. _____

   _____

   _____

5. Define the *hidden job market*. _____

   _____

   _____

(Continued)

6. How can job candidates prepare appropriate interview questions? _____

_____

_____

_____

_____

_____

7. List five illegal interview questions. _____

_____

_____

_____

_____

_____

8. Why is sending a letter to thank the interviewer important? _____

_____

_____

_____

_____

_____

Part III: Observe What You Have Learned

Job Hunting

■ Objectives

After completing this activity, you will be able to
■ list qualifications needed for employment in a child care center
■ list typical questions that might be asked during a job interview
■ identify types of responses employers prefer

■ Preparation

1. Arrange to interview a director of a child care program.

■ Setting

Place where observation occurred _____

_____

Name of director _____

Title _____

   Copyright Goodheart-Willcox Co., Inc.

■ The Observation

Identify what traits the director seeks in a potential employee by asking him or her the following questions. Record the director's answers below.

1. What educational experience is required for the various positions at your center? _____

_____

_____

_____

_____

2. Is previous work experience necessary? Why or why not? _____

_____

_____

_____

_____

3. Do you require and check references? Why or why not? _____

_____

_____

_____

_____

4. What personal qualities do you look for in an employee? _____

_____

_____

_____

_____

5. What are some questions you ask job applicants during an interview? _____

_____

_____

_____

_____

_____

_____

_____

(Continued)

Copyright Goodheart-Willcox Co., Inc.

Observe What You Have Learned (Cont.)

6. What kinds of responses do you prefer? _____

_____

_____

_____

_____

_____

_____

_____

_____

_____

_____

_____

_____

_____

7. Would you recommend a career in the child care field? Why or why not? _____

_____

_____

_____

_____

_____

Part IV: Apply What You Have Learned

1. For each pair given below, circle the item that most interests you. Explain your reasons in the space provided below the terms.

   classroom learning   hands-on learning

   _____

   _____

   working independently   working with others

   _____

   _____

   working with people   working with objects

   _____

   _____

(Continued)

Copyright Goodheart-Willcox Co., Inc.

working with people   working with data

_____

_____

working with objects   working with data

_____

_____

2. Listed below are some abilities that early childhood teachers need in order to carry out their responsibilities. Rate how you see yourself today in terms of having each ability. Use the following scale: 1=high in ability; 2=above average ability; 3=average ability; 4=low ability 5=no ability or experience in this area. For each item, write the appropriate number in the blank.

_____ leading group activities

_____ assisting children with activities

_____ communicating at child's level

_____ setting and enforcing limits for children

_____ providing comfort, nurturance, and effective praise

_____ offering constant and focused supervision

_____ handling or assisting with children's physical care tasks

3. For an item on which you rated yourself lowest, describe one way you could build your skills in this area.

_____

_____

_____

4. For an item on which you rated yourself highly, describe how this skill could help you advance in a career as an early childhood teacher. _____

_____

_____

_____

5. List five of your personal priorities. For each priority listed, explain why it is important to you. _____

_____

_____

_____

_____

_____

_____

_____

(Continued)

Copyright Goodheart-Willcox Co., Inc.

5. Place a check next to any of the following that are professional priorities for you:

_____ helping or providing service to others

_____ feeling a sense of accomplishment

_____ working as a team member

_____ having a leadership role

_____ gaining recognition

_____ earning a high salary

_____ being competitive

_____ working independently

_____ contributing to society through your work

_____ expressing creativity

_____ demonstrating responsibility

_____ having a sense of accomplishment

_____ building relationships

_____ sharing knowledge

6. For any item you checked, explain why you hold this professional priority and how it would serve you in a career as an early childhood teacher. _____

_____

_____

_____

7. For any item you did not check, explain why this is not a professional priority to you. Would it help or hinder you to have this priority if you were an early childhood teacher? _____

_____

_____

_____

Copyright Goodheart-Willcox Co., Inc.

Child Development Associate

National Credentialing Program

Dear Parents:

I am applying to be assessed for the Child Development Associate (CDA) Credential. The CDA Credential is awarded by the Council for Professional Recognition, located in Washington, DC. The Credential is awarded to competent caregivers and home visitors who have demonstrated their ability to meet the needs of children and parents on a daily basis.

The Council believes parents have the right to know that the individuals caring for their children are competent. Therefore, parents have an important role in the assessment of a person who wants to become a Child Development Associate. You can make an important contribution to a national effort to assure quality child care for young children by evaluating my work with your child and family.

As part of my assessment, I am required to collect the opinion of all parents who have children in my group. Therefore, I am asking you to fill out the questionnaire included with this letter. Your answers will be confidential. Please do not sign your name. Think about each question and answer it openly and honestly. Your specific comments at the end of the questionnaire will influence the outcome of my evaluation.

I would be grateful if you would return your completed questionnaire to me in the enclosed envelope (sealed) by_____ (date).

If you have any questions, please contact me at _____, or you may contact the Council hotline at 1-800-424-4310.

Thanks for your help.

Sincerely yours,

_____

CDA Candidate

CDA PARENT OPINION QUESTIONNAIRE

CDA Candidate's Name _____

> For each statement, circle the answer you think is best.
>
> YES = CDA Candidate does this.
>
> NO = CDA Candidate does not do this.
>
> N/A = Do not know or does not apply.

The CDA Candidate

YES NO N/A   1. Reports accidents or any first aid given to my child.

YES NO N/A   2. Requires my written permission to give any medication to my child.

YES NO N/A   3. Tells me about my child's eating, sleeping, and toileting/diapering.

YES NO N/A   4. Follows feeding instructions for my infant or for my child with allergies.

YES NO N/A   5. Allows my child to be picked up only by people I have named.

YES NO N/A   6. Reports to me about my child's play and learning.

YES NO N/A   7. Organizes toys and play materials so my child can reach them easily.

YES NO N/A   8. Provides a place for my child to store his or her own things and makes sure I can find the things I need to bring home.

YES NO N/A   9. Has enough toys and materials so children do not fight over popular toys.

YES NO N/A   10. Takes my child outdoors to play every day, except in bad weather.

YES NO N/A   11. Talks with my child frequently.

YES NO N/A   12. Listens with interest when my child talks and encourages my child to talk.

YES NO N/A   13. Helps my child learn to control his or her own behavior without spanking or using other harsh punishments.

YES NO N/A   14. Reads to my child often.

YES NO N/A   15. Provides many music, art, block, and pretend activities that my child can do in his or her own way.

YES NO N/A   16. Helps my child feel proud of what he or she can do.

YES NO N/A   17. Encourages children to enjoy getting along with each other.

YES NO N/A   18. Gives me the feeling that he or she is truly interested in my child and me.

YES NO N/A   19. Is pleasant and friendly to me.

(Continued)

Copyright Goodheart-Willcox Co., Inc.

YES NO N/A 20. Is available to discuss my concerns.

YES NO N/A 21. Asks me for ideas to use with my child, including activity ideas.

YES NO N/A 22. Asks me what I think is important in raising my child.

YES NO N/A 23. Talks with me about any fears my child has.

YES NO N/A 24. Maintains confidentiality; does not freely discuss my child or family in the presence of others.

YES NO N/A 25. Encourages me to visit at any time.

YES NO N/A 26. Lets me know of parent meetings and other ways I can become involved in the program.

YES NO N/A 27. Schedules conferences at times that are convenient to me.

Indicate language(s) you use at home_____

Indicate language(s) you prefer Candidate to use with your child_____

Please write your opinion about this Candidate's work with your child in the space provided.

Copyright Goodheart-Willcox Co., Inc.

Suggestions for Talking with a Child

1. Get down at the child's level and as close to his or her ears as possible.

2. Maintain eye contact with the child throughout the conversation.

3. Let your face and voice tell the child that what you are saying or doing is important, interesting, or fun.

4. Provide honest answers to the child's questions.

5. Use reminders rather than questions when children forget or refuse to follow directions.

6. Use short, simple sentences or directions.

7. Talk about the here and now.

8. Talk about what the child is interested in seeing or doing.

9. Say the obvious.

10. Everything has a name. Use it.

11. Put the child's feelings into words.

12. Use new words over and over again.

13. Take a child's short response and put the response back into a whole sentence.

14. When a child uses incorrect language, use correct grammar and restate what he or she was attempting to say.

15. Use a variety of sentence forms.

16. Expand a child's thoughts by adding more information.

17. Tell the child what you want him or her to do instead of what you don't want him or her to do.

18. Make statements that will encourage the child to continue his or her desirable activity.

19. Praise children for efforts as well as accomplishments.

20. Provide simple explanations to a child's questions.

21. Explain the anticipated consequences of specific behaviors.

22. Speak distinctly and use correct grammar.

23. Never talk about a child when the child or other children are present.

24. Talk with the children and not other staff during program hours, unless the conversation is related to immediate program activities.

25. Ask questions that will make a child respond with something other than yes or no.

26. Use phrases like "Tell me . . ."

Copyright Goodheart-Willcox Co., Inc.

Professional Connections

Magazines and journals are good sources of up-to-date information about early childhood education. You may find the following helpful:

The American Montessori Society Bulletin
American Montessori Society (AMS)
281 Park Avenue South
New York, NY 10010-6102
(212) 358-1250
amshq.org

The Black Child Advocate
National Black Child Development Institute
1023 15th Street NW, Suite 600
Washington, DC 20005
(202) 387-1281
nbcdi.org

Child and Youth Quarterly
Human Sciences Press
233 Spring Street, Floor 5
New York, NY 10013-1522
(212) 620-8000

Child Development and Child Development Abstracts and Bibliography
Society for Research in Child Development
500 East Huron, Suite 301
Ann Arbor, MI 48104-1522
(734) 998-6578
srcd.org

Child Health Alert
P.O. Box 388
Newton Highlands, MA 02161
healthalert.com

Childhood Education
Association for Childhood Education International (ACEI)
17904 Georgia Avenue; Suite 215
Olney, MD 20832
udel.edu/bateman/acei

Children Today
Superintendent of Documents
U.S. Government Printing Office
Washington, DC 20402
access.gpo.gov

Child Welfare
Child Welfare League of America (CWLA)
440 First Street NW, Third Floor
Washington, DC 20001-2085
(202) 638-2952
cwla.org

Day Care and Early Education
Human Sciences Press
233 Spring Street, Floor 5
New York, NY 10013-1522
(212) 620-8000

Developmental Psychology
American Psychological Association
750 First Street NE
Washington, DC 20002-4242
(202) 336-5500
apa.org/journals

Dimensions of Early Childhood
Southern Early Childhood Association
Box 5403 Brady Station
Little Rock, AR 72215

Early Child Development and Care
Gordon and Breach Science Publishers
One Park Avenue
New York, NY 10016
gbhap.com

Early Childhood News
2 Lower Ragsdale, Suite 200
Monterey, CA 93940
earlychildhood.com

Early Childhood Research Quarterly
National Association for the Education of Young Children (NAEYC)
1509 16th Street NW
Washington, DC 20036
(800) 424-2460
naeyc.org

Educational Research
American Educational Research Association (AERA)
1230 17th Street NW
Washington, DC 20036
(202) 223-9485
www.aera.net

Education Leadership
Association for Supervision and Curriculum Development (ASCD)
1703 North Beauregard Street
Alexandria, VA 22311-1714
(800) 933-ASCD;
ascd.org

ERIC/EECE Newsletter
University of Illinois
Children's Research Center
51 Gerty Drive
Champaign, IL 61820-7469
ericps.ed.uiuc.edu/eece/pubs/eece-nl.html

Exceptional Children
   Council for Exceptional Children
   1920 Association Drive
   Reston, VA 20091-1589
   (703) 620-3600
   cec.sped.org

Gifted Child Quarterly
   National Association for Gifted Children
   1707 L Street NW, Suite 550
   Washington, DC 20036
   nagc.org

Instructor
   Scholastic, Inc.
   55 Broadway
   New York, NY 10012
   scholastic.com/instructor

Journal of Family and Consumer Sciences
   American Association of Family and Consumer
   Sciences (AAFCS)
   1555 King Street
   Alexandria, VA 22314
   (800) 424-8080
   aafcs.org

Journal of Research in Childhood Education
   Association for Childhood Education International
   17904 Georgia Avenue, Suite 215
   Olney, MD 20832
   udel.edu/bateman/acei/jrce.html

Multicultural Leader
   Educational Materials and Service Center
   144 Railroad Avenue, Suite 107
   Edmonds, WA 98020

Report on Preschool Education
   Capital Publications, Inc.
   2430 Pennsylvania Avenue NW, Suite G-12
   Washington, DC 20037

Young Children
   NAEYC
   1509 16th Street NW
   Washington, DC 20036-1426
   naeyc.org

The following magazines are written for school-age children:

Babybug, Cricket, Ladybug, and *Spider* magazines
   Carus Publishing Company
   (800) 827-0227
   cricketmag.com

Highlights for Children, Inc.
   Box 269
   Columbus, OH 43216-0269
   highlights.com

Ranger Rick and *Your Big Back Yard* magazines
   National Wildlife Federation
   8925 Leesburg Pike
   Vienna, VA 22184
   (703) 790-4000
   nwf.org

Sesame Street
   Children's Television Workshop
   1 Lincoln Plaza, Floor 2
   New York, NY 10023-7129
   (212) 595-3456
   sesameworkshop.org

Stone Soup
   Children's Art Foundation
   P.O. Box 83
   Santa Cruz, CA 95063
   (800) 447-4569
   stonesoup.com

Turtle and *U.S. Kids* magazines
   Children's Better Health Institute
   1100 Waterway Blvd.
   Indianapolis, IN 46206
   (317) 636-8881
   cbhi.org

Other information may be obtained through various professional organizations. The following may be able to provide you with some resources:

American Association of Family and Consumer Sciences (AAFCS)
   1555 King Street
   Alexandria, VA 22314
   (800) 424-8080
   aafcs.org

American Association for Gifted Children
   15 Grammercy Park
   New York, NY 10003
   aagc.org

American Child Care Services
   P.O. Box 548
   532 Settlers Landing Road
   Hampton, VA 23669

American Educational Research Association (AERA)
1230 17th Street NW
Washington, DC 20036
(202) 223-9485
aera.net

American Montessori Association (AMS)
281 Park Avenue S, 6th Floor
New York, NY 10010
(212) 358-1250
amshq.org

Association for Childhood Education International (ACEI)
17904 Georgia Avenue, Suite 215
Olney, MD 20832
(800) 423-3563
udel.edu/bateman/acei

Association for Supervision and Curriculum Development (ASCD)
1703 North Beauregard Street
Alexandria, VA 22311-1714
(800) 933-ASCD
ascd.org

Children's Defense Fund
25 East Street NW
Washington, DC 20001
(202) 628-8787
childrensdefense.org

Child Welfare League of America (CWLA)
440 First Street NW, Third Floor
Washington, DC 20001-2085
(202) 638-2952
cwla.org

Council for Exceptional Children
1920 Association Drive
Reston, VA 22091-1589
(888) CEC-SPED
cec.sped.org

Daycare and Child Development Council of America (DCCDCA)
1401 K Street NW
Washington, DC 20005

International Reading Association
800 Barksdale Road
P.O. Box 8139
Newark, DE 19714-8139
(302) 731-1600
reading.org

National Association for the Education of Young Children (NAEYC)
1509 16th Street NW
Washington, DC 20036-1426
(800) 424-2460
naeyc.org

National Association for Gifted Children
1707 L Street NW, Suite 550
Washington, DC 20036
(202) 785-4268
nagc.org

National Black Child Development Institute (NBCDI)
1023 15th Street NW, Suite 600
Washington, DC 20005
(202) 387-1281
nbcdi.org

National Education Association (NEA)
1201 16th Street NW
Washington, DC 20036
(202) 833-4000
nea.org

Prevent Child Abuse America
preventchildabuse.com

Society for Research in Child Development
505 East Huron, Suite 301
Ann Arbor, MI 48104-1522
(734) 998-6578
srcd.org

Southern Early Childhood Association
Box 5403 Brady Station
Little Rock, AR 72215
(501) 227-6404